But after the gig...

But after the gig...

Tezz Roberts
with
Steve Pottinger

Ignite Books
2018

Copyright © Tezz Roberts & Steve Pottinger 2018

Tezz Roberts & Steve Pottinger have asserted their rights
under the Copyright, Designs and Patents Act
to be identified as authors
of this work.

All rights reserved.
Without limiting the rights under copyright reserved above,
no part of this publication may be reproduced, stored in, or
introduced into a retrieval system, or transmitted, in any
form or by any means (electronic, mechanical, photo-
copying, recording or otherwise) without the prior
written permission of both the copyright owner
and the above publisher of this book.

ISBN: 978-0-9932044-6-3

photos 1, 7, 11, 14 courtesy of Keith Harrison
photos 2 & 8 courtesy of Sebastien Marengo

Typeset by Steve at Ignite.
www.ignitebooks.co.uk

Printed and bound in the UK by
CPI Group (UK) Ltd
Croydon. CR0 4YY.

to Sadie, with thanks for
everything she's done.

Introduction

This isn't going to be a normal autobiography. You can be sure of that.

If you're expecting one of those books where the author tells you every last thing they've done in their life, where they dot every i and cross every t, then you haven't a hope. It won't be like that because I've done a lot, forgotten a fair amount of it, and – one way or another – I've been through the mill and back again, as the stories in here will make clear.

What's in here is the truth as I remember it. Things that happened, places I've been, bands I've played with. Adventures and misadventures. Stuff I did I probably shouldn't, and didn't do when maybe I should. Here it is. Warts and all. Enjoy it.

Tezz

Prologue	1
Stoke	5
Discharge	11
First Steps	17
Running	23
nigel	30
Singles	34
Leaving	39
Broken Bones	46
Subs	50
pete davies	55
Hospital	59
charlie harper	66
Shit	68
REM	73
bones	77
FOAD	78
Chicago	83
Social Life	87
Ministry	93
nigel again	99
Jolly Roger	100
Fall	106
Frying Pan	110
Fireworks	115

'burbs	119
casey orr	124
Regular Guy	126
Saints	130
Business	133
More Business	137
steve whale	142
Split	144
Houston	148
Speed	152
Jail	156
Freedom	160
ross lomas	164
Nuts	166
Kansas City	171
Loose Ends	175
Full Circle	179
jeff juniak	183
Drink and Drugs	185
Battered	189
Arrest	193
Toast Truth	198
Clean	202
sadie	206
Wrapping Up	207

Prologue

It'll come as no surprise – especially to anyone who knows me – to learn I've had a good few close scrapes in my time. I've sailed close to the edge way more than is sensible, and – mostly – I've got away with it. But of all the things that could have stopped my clock, you know what nearly killed me?

A couple of slices of toast.

It was 1984 going on 1985, and I was playing guitar in the UK Subs. When I first started playing with them I'd been on bass, but now I'd moved across to guitar, which was a massive transition, truth be told. I knew I had to be on top of it, and while I could just about pull it off, I also knew I wasn't that good. Yet. So I was under a lot of pressure, most of it from myself.

Anyway, we did this gig. I think it was at *Gossips* in London, but it could have been somewhere else. After all this time, it's hard to be sure, but it was one of those kind of popular after-hours-get-together kind of places, wherever it was. Charlie Harper sorted it out, and everyone was there. I saw all the old punkers. Wattie, and The Exploited, even someone out of Slade... and a bunch of people from where we rehearsed at Alaska Studios in London, they were there too. And there was a fight, of course – there was almost always some kind of fight.

It started because one of the guys who worked at this Alaska Studios went up and started messing about with my amplifier when we were playing. Now, I didn't mind – the guy knew what he was doing, so my take on it was *Go ahead, whatever.*

I'm playing the guitar and he's fiddling with the amp, and it's only getting better sounding as far as I'm concerned, because I'm new to playing guitar and still learning what to do. So he turns it up, or changes the tone or whatever it was he did, and someone took offence to that, and hit him. Not a band member, not one of the crew, just some random bloke who smacked him one. He started fighting back, and before you know it the whole place has erupted in one big fight, and that's it.

Gig over.

No-one's happy about it. I'm certainly not happy. So I did what I did when I wasn't happy – I found someone with a big bunch of drugs and took what was on offer. And no, I can't remember what it was, but then I didn't ask, I just snorted it all. Next thing you know – and this is hardly a surprise – I'm out of it. Flying. And then myself and a couple of other guys go back to Deptford, where I was staying with Deptford John, our roadie and bass player, to carry on the party.

John's flat was a small place with a balcony on the second floor of a tower block. You looked out, and all you saw was concrete. Concrete as far as the eye could see. All of bloody Deptford was concrete. Hardly a view that's going to help your mood. And I'm not happy anyway, because this had been maybe my second or third gig playing guitar for the Subs, and it hadn't lived up to what I wanted.

I figured I needed some toast. That was all I ever seemed to eat, back in the 80s. Toast, the cheap man's filler. A couple of slices of toast, and everything's going to seem a whole lot better. So I ask John, and John says

Well, we haven't got any bread, mate. You'll have to go downstairs and knock up my mate who lives on the first floor.

I was full of drugs and drink, and using the stairs seemed like too much effort. So I decided to take the quick route, and jumped over the balcony. I was two floors up, and if that wasn't enough, the basement entrance to the underground car park was right below John's flat, so I had even further to fall.

This was never going to end well.

I spent two weeks in a coma, then woke up in a hospital bed with everyone telling me I was lucky to be alive. Three weeks after that I was back on stage at the Lyceum, playing guitar. Did I learn from this? Did it stop me getting into scrapes? No.

But I never messed around with toast again.

Stoke

It was 1978. I was sixteen years old, living at home with my mum and dad and sharing a room with my brother. I'd left school – not that I'd ever spent that much time there anyway – with no qualifications. I had no real prospect of a decent job. The jobs that were on offer, I didn't want. I had asthma. I had bronchitis. I was dyslexic. And on top of all that I was in Stoke. Nothing ever happened in Stoke.

There didn't seem to be much to get enthusiastic about, if I'm honest. School, I'd hated every minute of. Some kids hate maths, but love sport. Or can't stand sport but live for science or maths or english. I hated all of it equally. I didn't want to be there, and I didn't want to learn. No-one asked why. No-one ever thought to explore what was going on, to the best of my knowledge no-one ever asked

Does this child suffer from dyslexia, Mrs Roberts?

and it was years later that I learned dyslexic isn't the same as stupid. Back in the '70s they just labelled me as thick and disruptive and probably breathed a huge sigh of relief on the days when I didn't turn up. So there were more and more days when I'd tell my mum I wasn't well because my asthma or my bronchitis was playing up, and fewer and fewer where I actually went to school. And if ever the school board man came round to find out why I wasn't in school, I'd just tell him to fuck off, and off he fucked.

The more I didn't turn up, the further I fell behind. Not that I cared. School was boring, and – like a lot of teenage lads – I was more interested in getting out of the house and hanging out with my mates in our little gang.

There was me, and Rainy, and this guy Mad Ant, and sometimes Bones and a couple of others tagged along too, so we were four or five or six teenage lads with nothing to do, filling our days by breaking into abandoned buildings – and there were plenty of them in Stoke – exploring them, and making them our own. We didn't trash the places, it wasn't about that at all, we just wanted a place for *us*, our den, somewhere where there were no grown-ups, no-one to tell us what to do, because we'd had enough of that already.

If there was a fireplace, we'd make a little fire, pretend we were explorers or outlaws or squatters, survivors of some kind of disaster, and we'd set booby traps on the stairs to protect us from enemies, villains, or wolves.

We'd always done stuff like this. When we were kids in Etruria, in the first place we lived, the back yard led straight on to the train tracks. And up the tracks there was a dump of abandoned army munitions and hardware. When we found that, it was like having a treasure island right on our doorstep. Even better than that. We had a choice between going to school, which we hated, or walking five minutes up the track and spending the day playing soldiers. What would *you* choose? It was no contest. No contest at all. We'd bunk off school, head up the tracks, and miss out on maths for the chance to play with busted-up bren guns and sten guns and helmets, all of them tossed together in this dump with no-one looking after them, no-one there to step in and tell us *No*.

I think lads all over the country were doing stuff like this. Looking for places they could burn off their energy without being told off for being a nuisance or making a noise, letting their imaginations run riot for an afternoon in a world where you were supposed to just knuckle down, do the same as everyone else, and get a job. There was no malice in what we were doing, none at all, but we got in trouble a few times, all the same.

One time, the police stormed into a building where we'd lit a fire, looking for someone who was on the run. But we'd set up our booby traps for just this kind of situation – although we'd expected monsters rather than cops, if I'm honest – and as planks and paint pots and lumps of masonry fell down the stairs, stopping the police in their tracks, we ducked out through a broken window and made our escape across the rooftops.

This was what passed for excitement in Stoke. Especially Stoke in the '70s. Especially Stoke in the '70s when you were young, and bored, and skint. There wasn't much else to do. I'd been to a couple of football matches, following Stoke away, managed to persuade my mum and dad to give me the cash for the coach and a ticket and some chips and a can of pop. To pack me off and get me out of their hair for the day, but that came to an abrupt end – a very abrupt end – after I went and got myself arrested.

It wasn't like I'd done anything. Well, nothing out of the ordinary, anyway. I thought when you went to a football match you were *supposed* to be a hooligan, and run around breaking shit. That's what I saw everyone else do. So I went to Blackpool with the rest of the Stoke fans and got myself arrested. For kicking a taxicab. Really. We were in the town, singing and chanting and making a nuisance of ourselves, everyone ran across the road and tried to push over a taxi, and I kicked it and got arrested.

As far as I was concerned, it was one of those things. Everyone's doing it, someone's going to get arrested. It just so happened the someone was me. That's the way it goes.

The problem was that this meant my dad had to come up to Blackpool by train to get me out of the cells, listen to the coppers tell him what a bad lad I'd been and how he needed to make sure I kept my nose clean from then on *blah blah blah* before they handed me over to him, and then march me to Blackpool train station to buy another ticket so he could get me home. All that didn't come cheap.

Was he pissed off? Yes he fucking was. He never said a fucking word from the moment he picked me up to the moment we walked in the door at home. He just gave me evils all the way.

The upshot of that little misdemeanour was that when I left school my dad was determined to make sure I got a job. Something that would keep me on the straight and narrow and take up my energy and my time. And that meant working in a factory, because everyone in Stoke worked in some kind of factory or another. My mum worked in a factory as a cleaner, and my dad worked in a steel foundry, melting steel and making moulds. So he got me a job there.

He did it for all of us. Bones stuck it for a while. My oldest brother's still doing it now – though in this day and age that's going to come to an end any time soon, with all this cheap steel coming in the country.

I lasted a week.

What did I hate about it? Everything. I wasn't ready for work, in any way. I'm not a lazy man, it's just – especially at that age – I wasn't prepared for it. My dad just threw me into it.

I was there for one week, and I learned that working in a furnace was hot and noisy, and it was dangerous too. There's no stopping that hot metal if it lands on you. It'll go straight through you, that shit.

And in the midst of all that heat and noise and danger, I was bored. Because I was nothing but a skivvy. There was no real job for me, but seeing as my dad was the main furnaceman and he'd had a word with someone about needing to find me something to do, they'd helped him out, and found me something. They gave me a broom and had me sweeping up a never-ending supply of crap.

It was a shit job.

All these years on, I can look on metal, and how people work it, and see that it's an art form. How they make swords and daggers, I can stand for hours and watch that. It's a beautiful art form, it really is. But at sixteen, I hadn't found the beauty of what metal really is, I was nowhere near ready to find that beauty yet. Especially when I was being asked to sweep up a never-ending stream of crap.

On top of that, I was already involved with the band, and the whole week that I was there, working in the furnace, being bored, all I could think was *There's got to be something better than this.*

Luckily for me, there was.

Discharge

Punk changed everything.

Now, that's hardly news. Even people who hated everything about punk at the time will nod and say *Oh yes, punk changed the world* as if they know what they're talking about, but unless you were there – and unless it touched you – you won't ever understand, because there'd been nothing anything like it before.

I'd grown up listening to rock, because that's what my older brother was into. It's what every one was into, although not every one was into the heavier end of it, like he was. I'd listened to the first Black Sabbath album, which was great, and I liked Cozy Powell's *Dance With The Devil* too, although I had no intention of becoming a drummer. I mean, who ever wants to be a drummer? And if punk hadn't happened, I guess I'd have carried on listening to rock, and that would have been that.

Instead, when I'm seventeen, I hear the Pistols. After that, everything changes.

There was this explosion of music. Like a pent-up fury finally finding a voice, and striking a chord with people. I remember buying *Never Mind The Bollocks*, taking it home, and playing it for the first time. I opened up our *Decca* record player, which was a tiny little thing you could pick up like a suitcase, with an arm and a turntable and a built-in speaker, took the record out of the sleeve, set it in place, and turned up the volume as high as it would go (which wasn't very high). I'd already heard the singles *'God Save The Queen'*, and *'Pretty Vacant'*, but this was the first time punk had happened in my home. We didn't have a big flash hi-fi, we didn't even have a telephone, and we'd only had an inside toilet since we moved from Etruria to Shelton, but nothing was going to stop us listening to music like this.

I couldn't get enough of it. And right there and then I knew I wanted to be in a band. I'd hated school, and I didn't see anything in the world of work which lit my fire, but this was something else. Luckily for me, my mum and dad were totally easygoing. They never turned round and said *Get a fucking job or you're out* like you see in so many other households. Not once. Not then, not ever. I wouldn't be here now, doing what I'm doing, if they had. I'd have had to knuckle down, and spend my life working. I'd have a trade. I might still be shovelling shit in a foundry, who knows?

Instead I was listening to punk. There were so many bands coming out. They might only do one single and disappear, but it was all fuel to the fire. I wasn't so keen on the American stuff.
New York Dolls? Nah. The Ramones? I saw them in '77 in Victoria Hall, Stoke-on-Trent. It was great, but then I saw The Stranglers too, and I liked them even better.

So, I was living on the dole – we were all living on the dole – and dreaming of being in a band. And when our little gang were hanging out, marching along canal towpaths, exploring derelict buildings, and getting up to mischief, we'd talk. We'd talk about being in a band and how it would change things, how everyone would know who we were, how we wouldn't be spending our time nursing a pint in The Sneyd pub till it was time to go home, or sitting in old barns in Alsager in the rain.

Don't get me wrong, we learnt more about life, and had more fun doing that shit than we ever did in school. But on its own, it wasn't going to ever be enough. If we were going to do something more than live on dreams, we needed to be in a band. If we were going to be in a band, we needed a line-up, and we needed a name.

The name came courtesy of the Pistols, and the little *Decca* record player in the front room. I was listening to *Never Mind The Bollocks* for the umpteenth time, and there was a line which just jumped out

just a discharge...

Even the way Lydon said it was perfect. That sneer and snarl. It was like a lightbulb went on in my head, and I knew *I want that!*

I didn't have a clue what it meant, but I didn't see how that really mattered. Still, it was better to be safe than sorry – we didn't want to give the band a name everyone would laugh at – so I thought I'd check what kind of reaction it got.

My mum was in the kitchen. What better place to start?

Mum, I've got a name for my band.
That's lovely, Terry.
I'm going to call it Discharge.
You dirty little swine! What d'ya mean? You're not calling your band that!
I am.
No, you're not! It's horrible! Bloody horrible!

And I thought *This is even better! Fucking hell!*

Next day, when our little gang were busy filling the empty hours by setting booby traps in abandoned buildings, I told the others that the band we'd been talking about forming now had a name. Discharge. I also told them I'd tried the name out, and it was suitably offensive. We were definitely onto something.

We hadn't rehearsed or anything, and we didn't have any songs, and we barely had any proper instruments, and none of us could really play, but those were just details. Nothing would stop us now.

Sorting out the line-up was easy. Rainy and Bones had guitars – cheap shit they could just about play chords on which they'd bought from *Kay's* catalogue or somewhere – so they were our guitarists. This lad Acko had a couple of drums, nothing you'd call a 'kit', but something to hit, even if it sounded like someone beating the daylights out of a couple of biscuit tins, so he was the drummer. Me? I was going to be the shouty bloke at the front because everyone else was too shy. Sorted.

Now we just needed a manager.

We didn't quite know what a manager did, but it seemed to mean people took you seriously. And that you got gigs and made money – which we all agreed was good. We also knew that they needed to understand the music business. But we lived in Stoke. Where were we going to find someone like that?

We knew there was only one place to go. The local record shop. There was this bloke Nigel who worked there, and we'd heard he had a hand in managing another local band, and seeing as we were in there a lot, listening to records, and talking about music, he was bound to jump at managing us, right? Next day, we met up, trooped down there, and asked him to manage us.

He looked at us.

Run the line-up by me again, lads.
Well, Acko's on drums... Bones and Rainy play guitar... and I'm the singer.
OK. There's one small thing...
Yeah?
You need a bass player.

Fuck. He was right. The first hurdle, and we'd fallen flat on our faces. The dreams of being in a band were over and we hadn't even had a rehearsal, done a gig, or had a chance to split up over that difficult second album. All we'd managed to do is look stupid. Fuck.

Nigel broke the silence.

I play a bit of bass.
You do?
Yeah.
Er... want to be in a band?

He shrugged. *OK.*

Discharge was up and running.

First Steps

Getting Nigel in the band turned out to be one of those right-place-right-time strokes of luck which helps make all the difference when you're just starting out in a band. Partly because it meant we had a bass player, and partly because it helped open doors we didn't even know were there, and which we'd probably have only tried to kick down if we had.

I think in our minds, now that we officially had a proper band with a name and everything – and a bass player too – nothing could stop us. OK, so we needed to get some songs together, and rehearsing would maybe be good at some point, but I don't think we gave it any more thought than that.

It never occurred to us that it's all well and good having a couple of catalogue guitars, but without amps to go with them you can't make any sound. And your drummer needs to have something more like a kit than some biscuit tins to practise on, too. And you need somewhere to set it all up and make a racket. Where on earth were we going to find any of that?

It was another hurdle we might have fallen at if it wasn't for Nigel. There was a band called The Veins, who were already established in Stoke-on-Trent, and he'd been in the same class at school as a couple of the band, and had something to do with managing them – probably because they already had a bass player. The Veins had jobs, they had money, they had gear, they had rehearsal space. In comparison to us, they were middle class.

We were scumbags, and they were well-dressed yahoos. But Nigel had a word with them and they offered to help us out. In our eyes, we were the real deal – even though we had no instruments, no songs and had never done a gig – and they were only *somewhat* punk. But fair play to them, they gave us a helping hand when we needed it, and we couldn't have done it without them.

I saw The Veins one time before they folded. At that point they were the biggest thing to come out of Stoke. They had a single out, and everything. *'Speed Of The City'* I think it was called. That time I saw them, Jenkins the guitar player was standing in a pool of beer, and I saw him have an electric shock off the microphone while he played. He was a big guy as well, and he had a fucking seizure on stage.

I always said The Veins weren't our cup of tea – and they weren't – because their music was a bit too melodic, and well-played. We wanted something noisier and more aggressive, and scary. And in yer face. Mind you, an electric shock's quite scary and in yer face, isn't it?

So, Nigel was the kingpin as regards The Veins helping us out. We knew of them, because everyone in Stoke did, but it wasn't like we were friends or anything. We were a bunch of nobodies just starting out, and they gave us access to their rehearsal space, their equipment, everything. Looking back, that was utterly amazing. A really generous thing for them to do. Without that we might never have got as far as playing a single note in anger. Even when the rehearsal place caught fire when we were in there, it didn't put them off.

The fire was nothing to do with us, by the way. Absolutely nothing. It was down to an electrical fault in the woodwork place downstairs. But we were in there rehearsing, and smoke started coming up the stairs, and we had to get taken out of there by firemen.

We practised whenever we could. After a while we had maybe five or six songs.

They were very basic. They were very cheesy. They were very badly played. But they were ours. Something we had made. We practised more. We got a little better. And then we got a gig. Our first ever gig.

Everyone has to start somewhere.

We started at Tunstall Town Hall. I assume it was down to Nigel. I can't see how else we'd have got it, but the truth is – after all this time – I haven't a clue. We didn't have a clue at the time, either. The gig was supporting a band from Liverpool called The Accelerators, so we told everyone we knew, and then on the day we turned up, expecting to use their gear.

The Veins had been happy enough to let us use their gear, so as far as we were concerned, all bands would be like that.

We were wrong.

We breezed in with our *Kay* guitars over our shoulders, assuming The Accelerators would let us use their gear, and they went *Fuck off*. Now, looking at it in hindsight, it's obvious you should always show up with equipment, or at least not show up with the assumption everyone else is there to help you out. But we didn't know any better, and we couldn't have done anything about it if we had.

Because we didn't have any equipment. We just had the *Kay* guitars. I'm not sure Acko even had a pair of drumsticks of his own.

I don't even remember if we did use their equipment in the end – I was the singer, so I didn't need it – but I can only assume we did do, because I know we played. But by then the damage was done, because the guys who were with us had taken offence when The Accelerators told us to fuck off. But that came later. First we had to do our gig.

We had our five or six cheesy, basic songs, and that was it. We told ourselves we were ready, but when I get up on the stage for the first time, I realise how terrifying the whole thing is. It's one thing rehearsing in a studio, but now there's an audience standing there, waiting, and I know I'm going to get up there and shout the words, develop a stage persona, and shit myself with terror, all at the same time. I'd only ended up being the bloke at the front because no-one else wanted to do it, and nothing has prepared me for this.

My heart is pounding and my stomach is in knots. I open my mouth to start the first song, and someone dumps a full pint of beer straight in my face. Suddenly I've more to worry about than struggling with singing. Suddenly I'm not that arsed about remembering the words. Because I'm fucking drowning. I can't breathe.

It's chaos. Absolute chaos. But we get through it all, somehow, and it's both terrifying, and it's a buzz unlike any other, all at the same time. I walk off stage feeling ten feet tall. Maybe even taller. I don't know it at the time, but no drugs come near what I've just experienced.

Years later I can say, hand on heart, that I've done a lot of drugs, but there's nothing – absolutely nothing – which comes anywhere close to matching the feeling that you get when you're showing off.

Then The Accelerators get up to do their set. And it all kicks off. As I said, our mates had taken offence when they'd told us to fuck off, and the upshot of that was they never got the chance to play the gig they'd come all the way to Stoke for.

I've one really vivid memory, like a photo in my mind, and it's of this guy I knew, Pete Johnson. I don't even know if he's alive now, but he was a humungous man, a mountain of a bloke, and he was on the stage strangling The Accelerator's guitar player. The guitarist's feet are off the ground, his guitar's dangling, and Pete's strangling him. I remember seeing that. Clear as day. I've a vivid photo of that, if nothing else. In fact there is nothing else. That *is* the gig for me. This guy's legs dangling, and Pete Johnson strangling him. For what? Because we couldn't use their equipment??

The gig ended in a ruck, as so many did. But when I got home at the end of the night I was still buzzing. Before we'd got on that stage, I'd been wondering how the fucking hell I was going to remember what words we had, and which ones went with which song.... I never reckoned I was going to end up drowning on someone's beer in the first few minutes I got on a stage, but I did. It was sink or swim, and luckily I swam!

We'd done our first gig, and it had gone all right. Yes, I got a beer thrown over me, but that was punk rock, that was what it was all about. Piss and snot and beer was just par for the course.

I had this feeling.
We were definitely on our way....

Running

That first gig turned my world upside down. I'd been out on stage in front of a crowd of people, and I knew I loved it. From what I could make out, they liked it too, which was even better, because I knew this was what I wanted to do. More than anything. I was sixteen years old. Why would I want to work in a foundry when I could get up on stage?

Dreams like that are a dime a dozen. What helped us make them real was the power of the press. Our local paper, *The Sentinel*, did a review of the gig. They must have been looking the other way when Pete started strangling The Accelerator's guitarist, because the review was positive. And that meant everybody wanted to see what we were about. Everybody wanted a piece.

Our second gig was at Longton Town Hall. It was us, and a disco. That was it. And there were four or five hundred people there, which was unbelievable. Nuts. All those people for a band who were rough and ready and had a handful of songs. Right then, we knew the ball was rolling. We just had to climb on board and hang on for the ride.

It wasn't for everyone, though. A little while later, Acko's girlfriend dragged him away. Nigel decided playing bass wasn't for him. I guess that happens a lot – the band someone's joined is just an extra thing they have to fit in their life, another thing to juggle, and they weigh it up and decide it was only ever meant to be a bit of fun and it's more trouble than it's worth. We could have folded there and then, but we'd had a taste of something better than working for a living, something we really wanted, and we weren't about to let it slip away.

Rainy moved from guitar to playing bass. So that was that covered. Finding a drummer might be a bit more tricky. And we knew we needed a drummer. But I had an idea.

Who's going to play drums, Tezz?
I'll do it.
You can't play drums.
Neither can you, but I'll have a go.
But what about the vocals?
Don't worry. I've got a plan.

There was this lad, Calvin, who'd been hanging out with us, carrying our shit and stuff. He was the nearest thing we had to a roadie, but he was a roadie who didn't have the honour of the title, a roadie who didn't get paid.

I couldn't see him being any cop as a drummer, but maybe he'd fancy taking over from me as the front man. I'd had enough of standing at the front and getting covered in piss and snot and beer. Maybe someone else could take that job. Someone like Calvin.

I asked him *Do you want a go at singing? I want to do the drums.*

He said *Yes.*

Next thing you know, the band has morphed from being a bunch of lads with two *Kays* guitars into the classic Discharge line-up, the one that first made its mark. The line-up as it is today, more or less. And I'm on the drums, out of range of most of the snot, and taking control of the sound.

Play to this.
It's a bit quick, Tezz.
Yeah? So what?

I was listening to stuff the others weren't listening to. I brought in different influences. But then we all brought in different influences. Calvin was all about Crass. He loved Crass, loved everything about them. I didn't. I kind of liked some of it

banned from the Roxy, ok
didn't want to play there anyway

that kind of thing. But a lot of their stuff, it wasn't for me. It wasn't very guitar-orientated, and I liked guitar-orientated music. I liked guitar and I liked drums and Crass wasn't really like that. All that military shit, I didn't dig it, but Calvin did. He went for it, all that dark weird shit they had, which Discharge incorporated. All that war imagery, Calvin took it. The rest of us didn't care, if I'm honest. We just wanted to make a racket, and as long as we could make a racket, some big unholy din, then Calvin could take it wherever he wanted with the lyrics. We didn't care. Apart from a couple of bits and bobs lyric-wise, we had no participation in that side of things at all.

We practised. We got more gigs. And we had an idea about how to handle the piss and snot and beer. Piss and snot and beer were par for the course back then, but if people were going to throw shit at us, I thought we should throw some shit at them. The afternoon of Calvin's first gig with us in Stoke-on-Trent, I went to the butcher's and got a big bag of offal. A big bag of entrails. Anyone wanted to gob on us, this'd fucking show 'em.

We went on stage, and the bag came with me. My plan was to hurl the entrails over the audience, especially if they were gobbing at us, but I was busy playing drums during the gig, so I didn't have time. At the end of the gig I pick up the bag, head to the front of the stage, and launch the contents into the air. All that stuff that's normally inside your body? That big pipe of guts you don't really expect to see, and certainly not at a gig? Well, I watch it fly through the air in slo-mo and wrap round some girl's legs like a bloody lasso. I'll never forget that. And I'm pretty sure she hasn't either. Something like that, I daresay it scars you for life.

It's impossible to imagine a band nowadays doing a gig and even *thinking* of throwing entrails at people. Or a venue thinking of letting it happen. Or people letting it happen to them. But these were different times. Violent times. Gigs could be violent affairs. And sometimes it felt like we were just another excuse for a punch-up.

For some reason we didn't mind. We'd start playing, and it'd all kick off, and we never questioned it. That was just how things were. It never stopped us playing, because we thought that was how it was supposed to be. You might as well try and stop a sunrise, or the tide. The kind of people that we attracted, they were that way inclined. Chaos surrounded them, so all we could do was *anticipate* it kicking off, and deal with it when it did.

It's worth pointing out that chaos surrounded us too. It still does, somewhat. That's why we have agencies working for us to say *Catch this flight. Be here at this time. You're going there.* Else it wouldn't happen. Even now, if we were left to sort it ourselves, it simply wouldn't happen.

So we knew, but we didn't really care, that when we did a gig it was going to be just pure fucking chaos. We knew that if we did a gig in Stoke, it would be a fight. If we did a gig out of Stoke, it would be a fight. Some of the crowd we'd attracted were older blokes, and they weren't that interested in the music. I don't know whether they came along because it gave them an excuse to push these younger kids around, or what. I'm no expert. I don't claim to see inside anybody's head, but you could see them thinking

This is better than football.
No coppers.
No blokes kicking balls.
No chance of getting nicked.
We'll just turn up and watch the band.
Well, we won't even watch them.
We'll just turn up and start throwing glasses.

Next thing you know, it's a full-on battle. Wherever we played someone put on a coach and came along for the fight. Pretty much all the gigs we did in 1980-81, they all turned into one big scrap. It was like everyone from Stoke-on-Trent who fancied a ruck would come to your town and whoever lived in your town and wanted to give us a battering, they turned up too, and it all kicked off.

We just happened to be in the middle of it.
Playing.

I remember we did a gig in Manchester, supporting the Subs, and that was proper scary. We started playing a song, and the place divided in two, each side bombarding the other with glasses. There were people tipping the pool tables over, taking their boots off, putting pool balls in their socks and using them as weapons. Scary. Scary. Scary.

Next thing I know, people aren't just throwing glasses at each other, they're throwing them at us. Glass is flying everywhere. I'm on the drums, and I've got glass in my mouth. I've got my cymbals angled down like some sort of shield to try and protect myself from the worst of it, and I've still got glass in my mouth. I remember thinking

This isn't a gig, it's a battle. It's a whole fucking venue erupted into a battle.

With all that happening, throwing a bag of entrails over the crowd was neither here nor there. But we stopped doing it. Not on grounds of good taste – because that didn't ever factor in anything Discharge did – but because it was summer. We did a gig out in Cottesmore, wherever that is, on a really hot day with a big bag of entrails in the back of the van. Drove out to this gig in the middle of nowhere, opened the doors of the van, and all these flies poured out. And the smell.

Unforgettable.

No more trips to the butcher's.
That was the end of that.

nigel

It was 1977, I was working in Lotus Records in Hanley, in Stoke-on-Trent, and the punk thing had just taken off. I was put in charge of singles, and because we were the first shop in Hanley to sell punk singles, they all started coming in. They being Rainy, Bones, Tezz, and their entourage. They hadn't got any money, of course. They never had any money, because none of them were working, and – officially – Tezz and Bones were still at school. But they still wanted to hear all the latest music.

Play us the new Chelsea single.
You're not going to buy it, are you though, Tezz?
No, I just want to hear it.

Unsurprisingly, being the first streaming service in Stoke made us a magnet for them. They were friendly enough – with a slight air of menace about them because they were trying to be punks – we let them listen to the tunes they liked, and they hadn't got much else to do. Then they formed Discharge. I was managing a group called The Veins who rehearsed in a top-floor room in Longton, and had their own PA. Discharge asked the Veins if they could use their space to practise, they said *Yeah* and Discharge used to go in and bash stuff out. I don't think Discharge ever paid anything for using the room and the PA, but then they had no cash, so how could they?

They were rehearsing, but they hadn't got a bass player, and it came up in conversation that I played the bass. Not particularly well, but that didn't matter.

Do you fancy it, Nigel?
Well, I'll give it a go...

We all lived in Shelton – I was living in a bedsit just down the road from Tezz, and Rainy wasn't far away – and after the rehearsals we'd walk home from Longton with our guitars and everything. This is why I was ten stone dripping wet, I think. An hour and twenty minutes walk, at ten o'clock at night, because none of us had a car. So we walked. That was what we did.

We kept rehearsing, and we kept walking home, and then we did our first gig. The Accelerators were from Liverpool and they were playing in Stoke and, somehow or other, we got the support slot.

The original Discharge line-up: Acker on drums, Tezz on vocals, Bones and Rainy on rhythm and lead guitar, and me on bass. The sound was poor, we couldn't hear each other very well, the gig wasn't particularly good. I was with my girlfriend and a friend who had a car, and when we came off stage I said *Come on, we're going. It's going to kick off here, and I don't want to be anywhere near it.* You could feel it. So I didn't see it, but I was told, that The Accelerators came on 20 minutes later, and their part of the gig never happened.

One of Discharge's entourage was this guy known as Screwy. Screwy Bolton. And he was an animal. He would pick a fight with anybody. We knew that Screwy and his mates were at the gig, and they weren't interested in the music or anything, they just wanted a ruck. The Accelerators came on stage, the singer came up to the mike and Screwy just lamped him one. That was it, game over. End of gig.

The second gig was at Longton Town Hall. Now, we rehearsed across the way in Longton, and we'd rehearse with the windows open, so wherever you lived in Longton you could hear us. That's my theory as to why this gig was packed. Heaving. 300, maybe 400 people there. But those were the times. *It's a punk gig, let's go!*

I'd been off work with really bad bronchitis, but I wasn't missing the gig – and I was rumbled by the deputy manager when I went into work the next week.

What were you doing Friday night?
Er....

But it was worth it. Support was Jonny Oatcake (a bit like Billy Bragg) and then we came on. What I didn't know was that the band had changed the setlist round. I don't know where I was when they made that decision, but I know I wasn't there. We're halfway through the fifth number, the song kicks in, I'm playing along. About twenty seconds in, I realise *I'm not playing the same song as you.* I can't hear what they're playing – we're using the Veins PA, and there's no monitors – so I muddle through. People love it. We went down brilliantly.

It was great.

Why did I only do two gigs? Bruno Brookes.

He was a DJ on Radio Stoke, and he'd heard the buzz about Discharge, and wanted to interview them, get them on his show. So it was set up for midday on a

Tuesday. And I couldn't get there, because I was working in Lotus, downstairs on the singles counter. Someone was off, and I couldn't get cover.

So the band turn up at Radio Stoke, and they've been to the local cake shop, and bought some custard tarts to eat. Reception is on the ground floor, but you've got to go up in the lift to see Bruno. Whether he was busy or simply decided to make them wait in reception, I don't know. But they got bored, and started throwing bits of custard tart at each other, and pretty soon they got thrown out.

I knew Bruno a bit. He called me over to Radio Stoke, and had a proper rant. He actually threw the phone across the room in anger. I thought *I'm not having this dwarf throw phones across the room at me!* I went back to Lotus, the band wandered in, and I said

I'm out. I'm not taking the shit for what you've done.

At some point after the Radio Stoke incident it's possible Tezz was accused of assaulting Bruno when Siouxsie played the Victoria Hall in Hanley. He might even have spent the night in the local nick. I leave it entirely up to you to decide if these two events were in any way related.

Singles

Despite – or maybe because of – the entrails and the violence we got ourselves a manager. A woman called Tania Rich. She was Rainy's girlfriend at the time, and she had something to do with the music business in Stoke, such as it was. I think it was her who put together the gig at the Rose & Crown, in Etruria, that time The Clash gig got cancelled.

The gig was supposed to be at Victoria Hall, in Hanley, which was *the* big gig in Stoke. We'd supported The Clash there before once, when I was still singer, and in the summer of 1980 we got the chance to do it again. But for whatever reason, The Clash pulled out. Everyone's showed up for the gig, but now there's no gig to go to.

Tania saw an opportunity. Down the road from Victoria Hall was the Rose & Crown. We were friends with the landlord, and we'd played there before, so she got us to ask him if we could put an impromptu gig on in the pub seeing as The Clash gig was cancelled.

You never know, it might bring a few folk down.
Well… OK.

We told a few people.
That gig's off, this gig's on. Come along!

They told their mates… who told their mates… and the whole thing just snowballed. Before we knew where we were, we were bringing the whole crowd from Vicky Hall down to the Rose & Crown, the place was rammed so full you couldn't move, the doors were open because there was no way you could shut them, and the whole street – from Victoria Hall to Etruria – was a sea of punks. The police turned up to keep an eye on things, but there was nothing they could do except watch the party and listen to the din.

It was a top gig. Did we get paid? I've no idea. If we did, it was probably in beer – if the pub had any left. And knowing us, it never occurred to us to ask for anything more. Everything was on the up. We could fill a street with people who wanted to see us. We had a manager. We were signed to a record label. And I was playing drums.

Me playing the drums was a big part of us creating our new sound. Because I'd been teaching myself to play, I'd been listening to lots of music, lots of different drummers, and I had lots of different influences. Philthy Animal from Motörhead for one, Pete Davis from the UK Subs (a phenomenal drummer who I recorded an album with later, when I toured US with the Subs and he was in the band – but that's getting ahead of myself) for another. I'd listen to them, and then I'd head into the rehearsal rooms and practice, and I'd always take someone with me, so that I was always under pressure to make it work, to get it right.

All that hard work paid off, because next thing you know, we've got this new sound. I've constructed this thing called the D-beat, which goes on to conquer all of Norway, and Sweden, and gets used by a load of hardcore punk bands. But I did it first. It gave us something special, something which made people stop and take notice, and Clay Records must have liked it too, because it helped our singles sell.

I can't remember whether we approached Clay, or they came to us, but I think it was Tania who got Mike Stone to come and see us. He had a record shop in Hope Street in Hanley, and he'd set up a small record label, and he had his ear to the ground for anything worth signing, so he'd have heard about this group of young punks called Discharge, and the racket they made, and the crowds they pulled. So Tania had a word with him, and he saw an opportunity, and signed us.

And that meant we got to make some singles.

We recorded the first single in some shitty studio somewhere near Stoke, or in Stoke. I can't remember the name. The point is that it was just a fucking closet somewhere. If you've never been to a studio, it sounds magical, exotic, and glamorous.

Trust me, this one wasn't.

We were in and out in three hours, and in that time we'd recorded *'Reality Is War'*, with that D-beat. I've realised over the years that what we chose as a musical style – if you can call it that – was the destruction of the blues scale.
Popular music uses the blues scale, but we went in between those notes, which no-one else was

doing at the time. We weren't doing it consciously, but it sounded dark and it didn't sound anywhere near normal, and it sounded a little bit like Black Sabbath did, and we loved that, so that's what we did. You can't sing along to our music, you won't hum it in the bath, or choose it for karaoke. You can't. It's horrible.

The best part about recording the single, the best part by far, was hearing it on the John Peel Show when it came out. He said

Now, there's discontent in Stoke-on-Trent. It's Discharge.

I felt incredible. John Peel had mentioned our band. And then he played our record. That meant everyone had heard of us, because *everyone* listened to Peelie. Everyone lay in bed at night with one of those tiny transistor radios, listening to his show. In those days long before the internet, when daytime Radio 1 was full of sweet, sickly, instantly forgettable pop songs, the two hours of his show were the only place you could hear the music you wanted, music you didn't even know you wanted till you heard Peelie play it. So hearing 'Reality' on his show made it – somehow – official. Made us real.

Even getting our hands on the single in Mike's shop on Hope St, and touching the actual vinyl, didn't match that. It was good. But being mentioned on John Peel was better. For now, though, Hope Street was ours. It was full of punks, like the Kings Road of Stoke, and we were the kings of it.

The world was ours for the taking.

We did three singles back to back, one after the other in rapid succession. One: 'Reality Of War'. Two: 'Fight Back'. Three: 'De-control'. All of them went straight into the independent record charts, which were the only ones that mattered.

We were the kings, right there, and no-one could touch us.

So what did I do?

I left the band.

Leaving

Playing in Discharge meant I'd done things I'd never dared to dream were possible. We'd supported The Clash. We'd supported The Damned and The Ruts on the *Machine Gun Etiquette* tour, which had been one of the best gigs ever. We'd made records and watched them make it into the charts. And we'd taken bags of entrails to gigs and thrown them at the audience – for a while at least.

Everything we wanted to do, we did. And we got away with it, mostly, because there was no-one there to stop us. All we had to do was make plans. Which was good, because plans were all we ever had.

On top of that, being in the band had been the first time in my life people had shown any appreciation for anything I'd done. I hadn't been to school much, and I didn't do much the few times I was there, so I'd never had teachers tell me *Tezz, that was brilliant!* At home, my folks were easy going, which had definite plus points, but they didn't gush over us. They just let us get on with whatever we were doing, and left us to it.

Put together, all of that meant I'd grown up with no signs of people being appreciative of anything I did. Ever. Until I started playing music. Then it changed. Suddenly I had people patting me on the back, telling me how great the band was, and wanting to know me.

All of which begs the question: why leave?

I've never dealt with boredom well. And I was bored. Yes, we were kings of Hope Street, but we were only doing sporadic gigs. There was no big tour or anything. Just a gig here and a gig there, and the rest of the time we were on the dole. We weren't up to much – or rather we weren't doing anything like as much as I felt we should be. I lived for the gigs, but between our gigs, life was more boring than ever. The others seemed happy enough with it, but I always used to think

There's got to be more than this!

I didn't want to be hanging around Hope Street with people telling us how wonderful we were. I thought we should be out doing something. Playing gigs. But there was always something holding us back. In Stoke, we were kings, but outside Stoke most of the gigs were only ever going to be support slots. But no-one would give us support slots, because we were just a fucking noise. A popular noise, but a noise nonetheless.

I was sick of all the violence at the gigs, too. The fact so many of our gigs ended up in fights probably didn't help us much, if I'm honest. Word got round that a Discharge gig meant every chance we'd bring a coach in from Stoke and end up destroying your town. Not only did that mean we'd go somewhere to do a gig and people would be waiting for us to bombard us with shit and get their retaliation in first, it also meant we got a reputation for being a hooligans' get together, and that was another thing that went against us.

There'd been nothing like Discharge. Nothing whatsoever. But when that first single came out, I didn't like it. What the others thought, I've no idea. They never said, and they never will. But I was listening to loads of different music, and I knew I wanted things to move on. I wanted Discharge to be a little more rock sounding, and that put me and Bones on opposite sides of the fence.

We'd always fallen out, ever since we were kids. It's inevitable. We were twins, which meant we were thick as thieves and the worst of enemies, at the same time. We'd hang out together, and then – out of nowhere – we'd be at each other's throats.

The worst fight I remember us having was when we were teenagers. It was a fight over which of us was going to the shop to get bread for toast (what is it with me and toast?). I thought Bones should go. He thought I should go. And the shop was literally at the end of the street. It wasn't raining or anything. We were just being bone idle and being teenagers and jockeying for power, flexing our muscles. It was a control thing. The sun could have been shining and it would have made no difference. It was all about making the other one do what we wanted.

So we started fighting, as we usually did. Like I say, we were always fighting over something or other. Only this time, each of us has knives. Bones has some shitty flick-knife, and I've got a big lock-knife someone had got me through some kind of hooligan network. A beautiful knife with a pearl handle. I loved it.

Neither of us mean to use them. We're fighting, wrestling each other, wanting to be top dog, and Bones is winning. We've each got a knife in our hands, and he's winning, and god knows how it happened, but he got stuck in the chest with it. I stuck him in the chest with my knife.

It was horrible. The wound wasn't big – just the width of a knife blade – but it was deep. The knife went in him like butter. Neither of us knew it at the time, but I'd punctured his lung. We've no idea know how serious it is – we're kids after all, when all's said and done – but we do know we've got to go to hospital. So we decide to walk there. No way are we having an ambulance turn up at the house, because then everyone will know something's happened and we'll cop it from our dad when he gets back home from work. So, we walk.

We walk past the shop which sold the bread we could have just gone and bought in the first place, turn right at the end of the street, and make our way to the hospital. And on the way there we make up this ridiculous story, because we know we've got to give some kind of reason why Bones – who isn't doing that well by this point – is turning up at hospital with a knife wound in his chest.

What do I say? What do I say? We got attacked by some bikers. That'll work.

No-one told me I was going to be questioned. No-one told me there was any kind of test. We get to the hospital, Bones is being seen by the doctor, and a nurse asks me

What happened to your brother?
Well, there were these bikers....

She calls the police. They're there in no time.

Right. Who are you? Where are you from? What happened?

I tell them the story and they don't believe a word of it. I can see them thinking

Bikers, son? Where's your Superman outfit, where's your cape?

Eventually, someone must have called my dad to tell him Bones was hurt. He turns up and asks what's going on, and I break down and tell them the truth.

I did it. There were never any bikers.

I know this means I'll be getting another thick ear off my dad when I get home. A real thick ear. I also know the knives will have to go. There will be no more knives in the Roberts household after this little caper. They'll go, and I'll be sitting in the corner for a week. Again.

Bones stays in hospital for a couple of days, because they've stitched him up and they want to make sure he's OK, and when he gets home I'm still sitting in the corner, in disgrace.
After that, if we were fighting, there are no knives. Only fists.

Which is what happened when we have the scrap which leads to me leaving Discharge, in Mike Stone's record shop, in 1980, when we turn it upside down.

Like always, it's about control. Just control. I wanted to improve, I wanted the band to sound how it sounds now. Bones didn't. Or I didn't think he did. Which was the same thing. And we were in Mike Stone's shop because we were on the dole and that was where we always hung out. We were in there every day. What shall we do? Where shall we hang out? Hanley, why not?

The fight starts over Bones' girlfriend, because he kept bringing her to the gigs. I didn't like the idea of other people being involved. It made the whole thing more like a fashion show, as far as I was concerned, that side of punk, with the hair and everything, and I didn't like it.

Bones had the big fluffy blonde crown. Cal had the perfect spikes and the perfect patch and the perfect tear in just the right place in the trousers, because he was a little more well-off than the rest of us. He was middle-class, and me and Rainy looked like what we were. Scum of the earth. Working class. Out of the alley.

I thought Discharge should be the four of us, just the lads. Tight. Together. No girlfriends. No-one else getting in the way. So we start arguing about that, and it escalates. That's how the fight starts. I decide to use my trump card, which is to go *Fuck it* and walk away. I want them to realise how important I am to the band, how much they need me.

I want some recognition from my own brother. I might as well want the moon on a stick. I've more chance of getting that.

So I go *Fuck it* and Bones is all nonchalant about it. That's how the fight starts. I want recognition, and he knows I want it, which means it's the last thing he'll let me have, so I probably hit him. And he probably hits me back. We start wrestling in the shop, throwing shit at each other. Records. More records. Whatever comes to hand. Mike isn't happy about us wrecking his shop, but there's not a great deal he can do about it. And when the fight is finally over, I go *Fuck it, I'm leaving the band.*

And no-one said *Don't.* No-one ever said *Don't quit the band Tezz, we're onto something here. You're part of it.* No-one said that.

I'm a proud man. So I thought *Fuck 'em.*

And I left.

Broken Bones

Bones wasn't going to ask me to re-join the band, and I wasn't going to swallow my pride either. So that was that. I wasn't in Discharge any more, and they found a new drummer, and carried on. They released an EP 'Why?' which went straight to No.1 in the indie charts, and headed off across the Atlantic for a huge tour of the States.

So be it. I'd got bored of looking at the back of their heads, anyway. Whatever I did next, I wasn't going to be playing drums. I wanted to show off. It's in my nature, I'd learned that. Showing off, and moving on. That's what I do. I'm always looking forward to what's next rather than looking back to what I've done. Living on past glories? That's bollocks. I've always gone forward, all my life. I've never looked back. And I didn't do it now.

I wasn't in the band? OK. I'd learn to play the bass. I'd learn to play the bass so that I could learn to play guitar. I'd change my point of view. Then I'd change it again. And I'd keep changing. I'd started off singing. Then I learned drums so that I could drive the music that we made. And now I'd teach myself to play bass so I didn't spend my gigs hidden behind a kit looking at the back of other people's heads.

I'd teach myself bass and something would turn up. I was sure of it.

Something did.

Bones left Discharge. And we teamed up again. Sure, this meant it would only be a matter of time before we found something to argue over, because we were always feuding over something. If it wasn't the music, it'd be something else. We were always bickering. We couldn't help it. So we knew that would be coming, somewhere down the line. But for now, we had a band, and it needed a name.

I read this article *Sounds* had written about Bones leaving Discharge. *'Bones has broken away from Discharge... blah blah blah... broken Bones....'*

Hmmmm, I thought. *Broken Bones. I like that. I'm going to use it.* So I wrote to *Sounds*, told them I liked their description, and by the way Bones and me are in a band and we're going to call it Broken Bones.

I was going to be on bass, with Bones on guitar. We got Stuart Duffy, who was a mate of Nigel's, in on second guitar, and then Bones found this guy Bazz to play the drums. I think he chose him for the way he looked, because he certainly didn't do it on his ability to play. Eventually Bazz turned into quite a good drummer, but when he joined us he was rough. I mean, *really* rough. I had to more or less teach him his way round the kit. But fair play to him, he picked it up really quickly, and he was quiet, and he showed up, and he drummed. Which was good.

We hadn't got a singer yet, but we started writing songs. I played bass and sang, and we even did a gig with me doing that – it was something I wanted to try out, something I wanted to get out of my system – and it was a bit more rock and roll, which I liked, but a bit clichéd sounding, which was definitely bad. We decided it didn't work. *OK, we've tried that, let's go back to something else.* That's when we got Nobby in on vocals, and hit a purple patch.

We started doing gigs, and now things were happening, because it was that time where the new UK hardcore scene was taking off, especially after Discharge had paved the way. So Broken Bones just sailed on it, and people paid attention to what we were doing. And it was more melodic – in a sense – than Discharge, because I was writing the tunes now and that meant I got to put my stamp on how we sounded. I wasn't just sitting at the back hitting things – those days were gone – I was writing the tunes, and that was what I wanted. I was writing the lyrics, writing the choruses. Then Bones would do his thing. We put it together, and it worked. This was it! This was what I wanted!

So we were getting gigs, people liked what we were doing, and then we put out our first single, 'Decapitated'. That came out on Jungle Records. Everything was looking really good. But that was never going to last for long, because nothing I'm involved in lasts for long.

I got offered a gig playing bass with UK Subs at the 100 Club in London. This was massive for me. If I had to pick my favourite bands at the time, three class bands whose work meant everything to me, it would have been the Pistols, Motörhead, and the Subs. I knew all the tunes. I loved their work.

Being asked to play bass with them – even for one gig down in London – was a huge temptation in itself, but on top of that they told me they wanted me to play on their next tour of the States.

Now, Bones had been to America with Discharge after I'd left. And I hadn't been. They'd done this big tour, all across the States, with loads of gigs – a tour people still talk about now – and I'd missed it. So straight away this fed into the rivalry between me and Bones. I was jealous. Bones hadn't talked to me about America. He never talks to me about anything. He didn't talk to me then, he doesn't talk to me about shit now. But he'd been, and I wanted to show that was good enough reason for me to want to go there too. I thought

I want to go there, I'll fucking do it.

Broken Bones was barely up and running, and I jumped ship.

Subs

I'm not sure how this offer to play with the Subs came about. I think it was via Captain Scarlet, the guitarist, but it might have been Deptford John, who was their roadie, and kind of a kingpin. The one thing I do know is that I didn't meet Charlie Harper till I went down to London for the gig.

We had one rehearsal. Just one. That was all it needed. I knew all the tunes anyway, and I was young and cocky and brim-full of confidence. That's my mantra: *Confidence is everything*. Go in believing you can do something, and you're more than halfway there. What can go wrong? Most of the time, nothing. Yes, Discharge and Broken Bones had been my bands, and now I was just going to be a hired gun, but that was neither here nor there – the Subs rehearsal was great, a piece of piss. They didn't say much, but I could tell they knew they'd got their man. I was in. I knew it.

We did the 100 Club show. It went well. Then, prior to going to America, we had some one-off European shows. I'm pretty sure one of them was in Spain. Why? Because we got pulled at customs going in. These things happen, it's no big deal. But someone in the band or the crew has decided to have a bit of a laugh with the new boy, and put a burnt spoon in my bag. The customs officers open it, find what looks for all the world like drug paraphernalia – confirmation in their eyes that at least one of this weird-looking bunch of freaks must be a junkie – and think they've hit the jackpot.

Next thing we know, we all get taken aside for a strip-search. This little joke has become a royal pain in the arse. We're all in some little side-room, taking our clothes off, and we can't help but notice that when one of our group – and I think it's only fair he remains un-named – when one of our group drops his trousers, he's got toilet roll wrapped round his knob.

What the fuck, mate?
He shrugs. *I've got gonorrhea, ain't I?*
Jesus.

There's green gunk dripping out of his knob and he's soaking it up with loo roll. The customs guys are disgusted. Suddenly they've lost all interest in the spoon, and can't get rid of us fast enough. They want us dressed and out of their lives, and they want it now.

We're only too happy to oblige. We don't get searched on the way out of Spain, either.

Funny, that.

Then, it's off to the US. My first time there. It was a long old tour. Something like two months on the road, which was a new experience for me, going from gig to gig in vans, covering a lot of ground and doing a lot of driving. We made it as comfy as we could, but as anyone who's done it will tell you, it's still a lot of your life spent staring out of the window of a van. We had a sound engineer with us, and two road crew, Deptford being one. I was playing bass, and Pete Davis – who's one of my idols – was on drums, so I was made up to be playing with him. It was Pete who coined my nickname on that tour, who first described me as his favourite nutter.

The northern nutter.

To be fair, he had a point.

Anything that was there, I was doing it. And you've got to be a bit nuts to do that, haven't you? If you're not when you start, you will be soon enough. But I was like a kid in a candy shop, and whatever I wanted, it was there. I was in America, I was English and in a famous band, and everything was up for grabs. There was drink. There were parties. There were people wanting to know me. And there were all the drugs in the world.

I was just a kid, and I wanted all of it, all of the time. Every day was the same: van, venue, gig, get fucked up on booze and whatever else was there. Repeat, and repeat, and repeat. Being abroad didn't mean any more than that. We stayed in nice hotels, but I was so wasted I didn't have a clue. Each day was a party, and I was young, and everything I wanted was being given me, on a plate.

It. Was. Great.

Now, all these years on, when I go somewhere I appreciate it. Instead of drinking, I get to enjoy the place I'm visiting. It's not as blurred as it used to be. I still don't get to see that much, because it's still van, venue, gig, but what I do get to see, I appreciate. Back then, it couldn't have been more different. I was the northern nutter, and it's hardly a surprise that sooner or later I ended up in jail.

We were in Lubbock, Texas. The gig was over, we were getting wasted, and we had some people come back to the hotel for a party. And one of them – and I genuinely can't remember whether this was a bloke or a girl – it turned out they had a wig on. I didn't know about it till I went to touch their hair, and this wig came off in my hand.

I'm having that!

I took the wig, and they took offence. We got in a row, and I ended up kicking them out of the hotel. A little later, they come back with the police, who throw me down, put the cuffs on, and drag me off. I wake up in jail, charged with assault, and I'm locked up there till the band can post bail for me and get me out. Did it mean I looked at what I was doing and decided to rein it in a bit?
Not at all.
No-one ever said I should. Charlie liked me, so that was good. I was doing my job, doing what was needed on stage, doing what I was told, and never arguing with the band. So, yeah, I was a bit of a nutter, and I was always fighting, always getting into some scrape or another, but – as long as I delivered on stage – that didn't matter at all. I was delivering, that was no problem, and I also had my eyes on getting the guitarist's role.

I was in the Subs to play bass, sure, but as far as I was concerned I knew how the guitar parts needed to be done, and I knew the guitarist wasn't doing them right. In my mind he was just a goth guy – his background was Siouxsie And The Banshees – thrown into a hardcore situation. He'd got all these effects going on when he played, and people weren't liking it. The fans wanted something more like Nicky Garrett, who's one of my favourite guitar players, and this guy was a bit too goth. But then Charlie was a bit goth on that tour, too.

Do I enjoy the tour? Yes. And no. I'm out in the States with a famous band, and I'm having a party, so that's obviously good. But at the same time, even though I'm the new boy in the band, I think it could be better. The guitarist's ok, but he's not brilliant, and I'm convinced I could do a better job.

I want his gig.

pete davies

I properly met Tezz when the Subs toured Norway in March '84. They flew out, I joined them in Bergen, and we did the first gig. No rehearsals. Typical Subs.

This is the guitarist.
Hi.
This is the bass player.
Hi.

3...4... and off we go.

At the beginning of the tour I didn't know who Tezz was. Our guitarist, Captain Scarlet, was more crazy than he was. He's indestructible. On his fifth liver. That wasn't a good example for Tezz, I suppose, though we didn't know that. At this point he was fairly straight and sane and smiley. That deteriorated over the next four months.

We did two gigs up in the Arctic Circle, Bodø and Tromsø. Then we went to America for a huge tour. Two months on the road. A lot of miles. We started on the east coast and did the usual shows, then the roadies drove to California with the gear, while we had one gig in Trenton, NJ. We had one day off, got drunk, and got to the gig the following day. With no roadies.

The dressing room is upstairs at the far end of the venue, the stage is downstairs. No quick way between the two. All day there's a lot of drinking going on – we've been given pitchers of beer – and when we've got ten minutes till our set starts Charlie, myself, and Captain go down to the stage.

The intro comes on – we're using something from *Fistful of Dollars* – and when that finishes, bang! we're straight into *Emotional Blackmail*. During the intro, Tezz strolls across the stage, holding his pitcher of beer. He walks over to the amp, which the venue has supplied.

Where's me guitar then?
We've no roadies, remember?

His bass is in the dressing room, which is above our heads, and we've got thirty seconds of intro left. Off he wanders. We start the opening track, and a little while later Tezz walks across the stage in front of me, carrying his guitar case, with this gleeful smile. He opens it up, takes out his bass, has a swig of beer, and joins in. By the time the gig ends he's battered. He's got his head in the bass cabinet, lying on his back, just strumming away.

Amazingly, he's actually strumming the right notes.

He was a great bass player. Musically, Tezz can play.... anything. He plays guitar. He plays drums. He plays really good bass guitar. I mean, his bass playing's *really* good. We recorded one show outside Chicago, you can hear it on *Gross Out USA*. Actually, Tezz makes one howling mistake on that album, plays a bum note just when you really wouldn't want to make a howling mistake, but every night, he was right on it. Even when he was really drunk.

I really liked him. He was nice and he was crazy. He did these crazy things. We could share daft jokes, and have a laugh, and it's quite childish, but you need that when you're in a van for 200 miles. As a mate and a companion, he was great. Just some days something veered off, some days he was worse and you gave him a bit more room, and then he'd come up giggling because he'd done something atrocious....

Because there was a darker side to Tezz. I was sharing a room with him on the whole tour, and some days there were things he was coming out with that just weren't right. He never took it out on us, but in his head there was confusion and frustration.

In Dallas, some girls put us up for a couple of days. When we headed off in the van, Tezz told us he'd stabbed their water bed before we left. *Fuck's sake, Tezz, they've given us somewhere to stay for two days, and been nice to us, and then you do that? Why?*

I didn't think of him as violent, but he started using violence. He was getting frustrated. He could be quite beastly to older women who'd tagged along. Scarlet would do that a lot, but he was generally misogynistic. Tezz, it was as if specific people set him off, but you'd never know who would do it. Or when. You never saw it coming, but suddenly, he'd single out a woman for something.

When we got to Lubbock, Tezz got himself arrested. He'd got off with a girl, her boyfriend turned up, there were words, and Tezz kicked the car door closed on her legs. That's a good reason to get arrested, and the police were happy to oblige. We all went down to the sheriff's office, chipped in to pay his $600 bond, and bailed him out. *Why the hell d'you do that, Tezz?* but there was no good answer. Just craziness. A real craziness he couldn't rein in.

The trouble with gigging is you do the gig, and that's one hour, and then there's the rest of the day. It's easy to have arrested development, where you have this strange life where everything's focused on that one hour in the day.

Some people – like Charlie Harper, who does it all the time – are really well adjusted to that. And then some people, its's just not that simple. But they still need it, and they still want to do it all the time. And back then, that was Tezz. Playing great bass, then doing something beastly and coming to tell you about it, grinning and laughing.

I got on really well with him, all the time. I couldn't fall out with him. I wouldn't. He needed help, and he needed friendship, and I was happy to give it.

Even now, when I see Tezz playing, he still looks great. He just loves doing it, he always has done, and it's the best thing for him.

Hospital

I toured all round the States with the Subs, having a great time, but fantasising about taking over on guitar. I've got that well and truly in my sights. For now, I'm playing bass, and after that tour of the States there's even a gig where I play drums for them, in Malta. I don't remember much about it, but there's a video of the Subs playing the Olympic Auditorium in LA, which is a massive venue, and Charlie saying

We've got Tezz on bass from Broken Bones, and he's going to play drums – 'cause he's from Discharge as well – on the next show we do after this, in Malta

so I know it happened. Anyway, not long after that we come back to the UK, and my dreams come true, I get the gig. I'm in the Subs, and playing guitar.

I've only just learned to play chords. Looking back, I'm really naive. But with my naivety comes confidence. I've hardly ever been short of that. If you've got confidence – especially in music – everything's going to fall into place. *Confidence is everything*. The ability can come later. I'm still finding my feet as a guitarist, but I know I can front it. It'll all be fine.

At first, it is. Then there's the gig at *Gossip's*. And I jump over the balcony to get some toast. Which wasn't my brightest move. My story could easily have ended there and then. I know how lucky

I am to be sitting here now, because if I'd have landed just a little bit differently that night, I'd be dead. Luckily, I was so drunk and drugged up when I hit the ground that I was just... floppy. That saved me, I think. Being floppy. I may even have bounced a little bit. I don't know.

What I didn't know either was just how much trouble this caused. While I was lying in a hospital bed in a coma, Deptford and everyone else who'd been in the flat that night got nicked. They were in jail, and my wife – who was convinced, like the police, that someone must have pushed me off the balcony – had come down from Stoke to sit at my bedside. When I eventually came round, there she was, with a copper.

His first question came as a bit of a shock.

Who threw you off the balcony, Mr Roberts?
What?!
Who threw you off the balcony?
No-one. I did it myself.

He looked sceptical.

You did it yourself?
Yeah.
Why?

I couldn't remember. Why had I done it? Then I saw a plate next to the bed. On the plate was a slice of toast. I saw that, and it all came flooding back. Lots of drink, too many drugs, wanting toast, and deciding to take the quick route to the flat below.

I explained this to the copper, who looked at me like I was an idiot. He probably had a point. My missus – who'd been convinced I was the victim of a vicious crime – was furious with me, too. But I'd jumped off the balcony, so I had to take the rap. No-one was going to be particularly sympathetic. No-one. The copper, my missus, Deptford and his mates, none of them were happy about the trouble I'd caused, and I can't say I blame them.

As soon as I could, I discharged myself from hospital. My head was the size of a melon, and my whole body was black with bruising, but apart from some stitches in my mouth from where I'd put my teeth through my lip when I hit the ground, I had no visible injuries, which was pretty incredible, given what I'd done.

No visible injuries. But I was in a lot of pain.

I went back to Stoke, because staying at Deptford's wasn't an option any more – he really didn't want to see me for a while. I was back in Stoke, and black with bruising, and everything was difficult. Everything. I couldn't walk, for starters. I could only hobble. But then I had just jumped off a balcony and fallen thirty feet onto solid concrete, so what did I expect? I was lucky to be here at all.

If I was going to get better, I'd just have to work at it. Every day I'd hobble from Shelton to Hanley, to the record shop there, which was maybe five miles there and back, to see some friendly faces and have a chat. The first time I walked in, the conversation stopped.

Fuck's sake, Tezz. What happened to you?

So I told them the story. And I'd exaggerate a bit, obviously – because a good story is all about exaggeration. The skill in telling it is to know how much you can exaggerate. And in this case, I really didn't need to do too much. They only had to look at me, or watch me hobbling up the street on my way back home, to see what had happened.

I had to teach myself how to walk again. And I had to teach myself how to make chords, too. When I first came back to Stoke I couldn't even think of playing guitar because I couldn't make any chords. I couldn't even bend my fingers into shape. I had to learn how to walk, and learn how to play guitar, and if I didn't manage to do both of those I was stuffed. I knew that.

So every day I had to stand up, which was hard. And I'd have to bend my fingers into shape so I could make chords, and that was hard, too. But both of these had to be done, and they had to be done together. There was no point in me practising chords and playing guitar sitting down, even if that was a load easier, because I knew that when I got back to playing gigs I'd have to stand. I'd have to move around the stage. I'd have to look the part.

Every day I stuck to my routine.
Every day I'd hobble to the record shop.
Every day I'd stand up and put on the guitar.
Every day I'd bend my fingers into shape.

It was difficult. It was painful. But, slowly, it got

easier. Each day I got a little nearer to my goal, which was to be able to play guitar with the Subs again. There was a gig at the Lyceum, and I was determined I was going to be there.

I'd played the Lyceum once before, when I was in Discharge, playing drums. We'd been opening up for U2, who went on after us, and Slade, who were the headliners. Quite a combination, to be honest. Pretty bloody weird in itself. But the weirdest thing about the gig – and the thing I remember above all else – is that this was Calvin's first big gig, and he was nervous like you wouldn't believe. In the end, he was so nervous he just vomited, on stage, during our set. The techs, and U2's techs in particular, went bonkers.

Clean that up! Clean that puke up!

Our driver, Martin Edwards – who designed the three skulls logo for Discharge but never got credited for it, and was a great artist and a top bloke – he came on stage with a mop. He's mopping all this vomit from round the monitors where Bono's going to be standing later, but it's chunky vomit, and it's not going anywhere, and Martin's just pushing it round the stage from one place to another when all's said and done. Yes, he's giving it his best shot, but it really isn't helping. Then the mop handle breaks. And Martin gets a standing ovation. The place erupts in cheers! Which beats anything we've managed, because there are maybe two hardcore punks in the place, and for most of the people there Discharge isn't their cup of tea.

Bono hated us. *Who's put these fuckers on??*

We did an encore anyway. Garry Bushell reviewed the gig for *Sounds* and said we encored to two farts and a cough at the front! He was right. And we never crossed paths with U2 and Bono again, but that's their loss, and I'm sure they regret it.

So I've got good memories of the Lyceum. And now I'm going back there with the Subs. My wife comes down to the gig with me, and it's the first time either of us have seen Deptford or Jim Moncur since they got locked up and accused of trying to kill me, so it's all a bit awkward, to say the least. But Jim's crew, so he doesn't get to say who's in the band, and Deptford's taken over on bass since I've started playing guitar, so he's kind of got the gig because of me. But it's all a bit complicated. And we're not talking about the balcony or the toast or what happened. Not at all.

It's just three or four weeks since I took a header off the balcony, and I'm still a long way from being well, and I'm under a lot of pressure. Again, and as always, it's mainly from myself. We're playing our set, and I'm managing to do all right, despite the pain, and then I break a string.

I'm playing my Gibson SG, and the string breaks, and all I can think is how something's gone wrong – again – and I launch it. I properly launch it.

The Gibson sails through the air, crashes back to the floor, and breaks into three pieces. It's an £800 guitar, and I've trashed it. Back then, £800 was a lot of money – I mean, it's a lot of money now – but in 1984 it was a *lot* of money. I know roadies say there's nothing you can't fix with a roll or two of gaffer tape, but when I look down at what's left of the Gibson I think to myself *That's beyond saving*. There's nothing I can do about it, anyway, because I'm still getting over my close encounter with Deptford's concrete, and I can't even bend down to pick the bits up.

Someone gives me another guitar.
The gig goes on.
The Gibson ends up in the bin.
Deptford and I never talk about the balcony.

A little while later, we fly out to America. Time for another big old tour.

charlie harper

I first met Tezz in Manchester, in maybe 1979 when Discharge exploded on the scene. We did a show together and the place just erupted.

We didn't really know the band till then, but we had a good drink and a laugh in the wreckage of what was left of the ballroom after the gig.

The next time I remember we played together again was at London's Greyhound music venue. This must have been one of the first Broken Bones shows. I had a new guitar man called Captain Scarlet, they had a new front man called Nobby. Once again the place exploded, and we both got signed to a new record label, Jungle records. We loved Broken Bones and had them as our main support at London's 100 Club.

Next thing you know, we were off to the USA together, with Tezz on bass. And if you want to know how that went, just take a look at the cover of the UK Subs *Gross out USA* LP, that says it all..

After a squark at Gossips in London celebrating the fact we're off on a tour the next day, its 3am and I wobble home. The rest of the band go to party at someone's flat and get high. Then, when they're leaving, Terry somehow manages to fall over the first floor balcony and is taken to A+E.

He doesn't recover consciousness until three week's later. Three weeks. By then Scarlet and Jim are in jail for attempted murder and we have a tour. It's not what you'd call ideal preparation.

There are a thousand stories about Tezz. Some good, some bad, some downright ugly – we all laugh about them now even if we didn't at the time – but if Terry is your friend, he will take a bullet for you.

If I had to sum him up in one word, or one phrase? Simple. Try this.

Tezz is a rottweiler.
But with mega talent.

Shit

It was quite early in the tour – we're just five gigs in – when I succeeded in blotting my copybook. The tour's supposed to be two and a half months long, but this is the last I see of it. We're in Toronto having just come out of Buffalo. It's a ball-ache getting into Canada, 'cause we're a freaky bunch of fuckers – almost all of us have got some kind of criminal record or another – and the Canadian border guards don't like us. Not one tiny little bit. But we get in, eventually, and go to Toronto. And the gig there is nuts. Bodies are flying everywhere. People are having a great time. It's a good night.

I'm enjoying this tour of North America more than the first one. This time, I know what to expect, and I know I'm going to have fun. Sure, I've got to pay a lot more attention to what I'm doing while I'm on stage – I'm playing six strings not four now – but I'm giving the punters what they want, which is more energetic guitar than they got the last time the Subs came to town. What I'm playing is more like what Nicky Garrett played, so they're liking it. And I'm living up to being the northern nutter, drinking and partying and doing whatever I want, because – well, because it's fun. As simple as that. But in Toronto, it turns out to be my downfall.

We finish playing, and I start partying, celebrating our one and only gig on our one and only night in Canada, because next day we've got to go back through the border where the border guards will – undoubtedly – be only too glad to see us out of their country, and then we'll be back in the USA, criss-crossing the country from one venue to another. I've got just one night here in Canada, and I'm happy to drink whatever's put in front of me, take whatever I'm offered, and talk to whoever is there.

If you want to turn one night in Canada into a week, read on, because this is the way to do it.

By the time we get back to the hotel, I'm so wasted I can only see the lobby. But I'm not going to let that stop me. Not when there's drinking and partying to be done. One by one everyone turns in. Did I sleep at all? I don't know. Not much, if I did. And early next morning – and it's fair to say I wasn't really in my right mind, wasn't straight, because what I did next wasn't a thinking man's thing, and god knows who was in control of things at this point – early next morning I have a big old shit into a plastic carrier bag and go banging on doors, waking people up.

Deptford opens his door a chink, sees me, knows I'm up to no good, and slams it shut instantly. I bang on another one.
The tour manager opens his door, and I let him have it. I've got a huge turd in a plastic bag, and I just hit him round the head with it.
I think it's fair to say he wasn't expecting that first thing in the morning. Who would? He freaks out – as you would. It was a horrible thing to have happen, whichever way you look at it. Not that I thought that at the time, but as I say, there wasn't

a right lot of thinking going on, not on my part. I was full of drugs and booze and devilment, and it never occurred to me I'd done anything wrong.

I was way too fucked up to have thought about what I'd done. And way too fucked up to have thought about the repercussions of it, either.

What I'd forgotten was that the tour manager had all our passports. When we'd come in through customs into Canada he'd collected all the passports, because dealing with border officials and customs officers and smoothing over the difficulties of getting a bunch of freaky fuckers from one country to another was part of his job, and seeing as we were heading out of Canada a day or two later, he'd hung onto them.

And with him not being entirely happy about having a warm turd wrapped round his neck, before we left Toronto, he stuck my passport in an envelope, addressed it to the consulate, and put it in a mailbox. I have no idea about this, of course, but then I don't have much idea of anything at this point. We get in the van, drive back to the border and... I've no passport.

What have you done with it Tezz?

And me not thinking straight, which was hardly a surprise after a long night of partying, I couldn't remember whether I'd given it him – which I must have – and whether he'd given it me back. He claimed he had. I hadn't a clue. So everyone else goes through the border, and I have to go back to Toronto, thinking my passport must be there. Maybe it's in the hotel room. Who knows?

So I use what little money I have to get back to Toronto, and check the hotel. No passport. And nowhere to stay, either, which isn't good. Fortunately, I've got the number for these girlfriends of Wattie's who came to our gig the night before, so I give them a ring, tell them I've lost my passport, and hook up with them. They take care of me, give me a bed for the night, and next morning I contact the British consulate, explain – again – that I've lost my passport, and ask them for a replacement. That's going to take a while to be arranged, and in the meantime I'm staying with Wattie's girlfriends, because there's nothing else to do. I have no idea what's happened with the passport, I just know I haven't got it.

Have I lost it? Maybe.
Has it been stolen? Perhaps.

Then the consulate rings.

Mr Roberts?
Yeah.
We've got your passport.
That was quick.
No, we've got your old passport.
The one that's missing?
It isn't missing.
It is.
It isn't missing now.
Where is it?
We've got it.
I see. (I don't see at all) How did you get it?
Someone mailed it to us....

And at that point I've got my passport back, but I have no idea at all how it got there. Something's happened, that much is clear, but I'm as far from an explanation as it's possible to be. Maybe some kind soul found the passport somewhere and decided to post it to the consulate. I mean, no-one could possibly want to mess me about so much that they'd put my passport in an envelope and post it to a consulate so I can't carry on with a tour across America with a band where I'm playing guitar. Would they?

You won't believe how long it takes that penny to drop. But it's a long long long time later when I suddenly find myself thinking

What would you do if someone hit you round the head with a bag of poo?

I'd have done worse than put his passport in a postbox, believe me. A lot, lot worse.

REM

The good news is, I've got my passport back. The bad news is, I'm stuck in Toronto. I've been there a week or more, and I've no idea how I'm going to get home, and then my old friend Lady Luck steps in.

REM are playing in town. These girlfriends of Wattie's who are looking after me know REM's tour manager, so before the gig they go along to the hotel to meet him, and they take me with them. I don't know if they went there *specifically* to supply him with drugs, but... let's just say it's a possibility.

It's a possibility because – while I can't for the life of me remember whether I went to the gig – I know I met Michael Stipe. I was in the hotel lobby before the gig, and he came up to me, sniffed the air, and said *I smell cocaine.* I thought

Fucking hell, he's got a keen nose!

I'd just come down from the hotel room after doing a big fat line with the tour manager, so he had me bang to rights in fairness, but it was still kind of weird. The only thing I remember about REM, the one sole thing I can tell you with any conviction, is that Michael Stipe has an incredible sense of smell. I can't remember anything apart from that, but they just wipe my slate, drugs do, so it's something of a miracle this memory made it intact through all the years.

Did I watch the gig? Like I say, I've no idea. Not the foggiest. I do know that I spent the night on their tour bus while the band stayed in the hotel, and next day when they drove back across to Buffalo, I went with them. I don't think I even got off the bus at the border, I just sneaked in.

Lucky. If it hadn't been for that tenuous connection – REM happening to be in town and Wattie's girlfriends knowing the tour manager – I'd have been fucked. Up shit creek in Toronto without any kind of paddle. As it was, I was lucky. But then things generally turn out right, in the end.

Or – as you'll see later – they don't.

Courtesy of REM and a decent-sized helping of luck, I'm back in the USA. They get me to Buffalo, and from there – somehow – I get home. I can't remember how, whether I got a flight (which seems unlikely, as I had no money) or whether the Subs sent me the ticket, or orchestrated something, or whether I somehow figured it all out on my own so that I could come back to the UK (also unlikely, as I wasn't much for figuring things out at the time). My best guess is that the Subs had a flight back in my name and let me use it, and I flew back to the UK while they carried on with the tour.

If there was one thing I knew for sure, it was that I'd lost that gig. Definitely. All thanks to a moment of madness with a still-warm turd.

I land back in the UK and consider my options.

I've lost my place in the Subs. I've nothing in London, and nowhere to stay. Deptford's off in the States playing bass, and if he was here he wouldn't want me round at his anyway. If I ever had any bridges on the go, I've burned them.

There's only one thing for it.
I go back to Stoke, and rejoin Broken Bones.

It might seem like a strange thing to do, to go back to a band I'd dropped without a second thought when my chance came to play with the Subs. And it might seem even stranger that – given how quickly I came back again – the others let me in, and didn't tell me to sling my hook. But that's what happened. Luckily for me, my brother's a pushover, so I can do what I want. And the others, well, I think they knew a good deal when they saw it. Bones might have had the name and the look, but I was the songwriter and the driving force. They knew that, even if they didn't want to say it.

They didn't write any songs while I wasn't there. Bones and myself, when we're together in a band, it's a certain magic that him and me have together. I'll push him to get the best out of him.

No, that's not good enough. Do something else. Put that in. Do that again.

No-one else will push him like that. They'll just sit back and let him get on with it. The two of us together, we're like a hardcore version of the Gallagher brothers. He won't work unless someone's pulling his levers. And I'm that man. He can't do it unless someone's giving him grief, and no-one gives him grief except me. Even now, it's still the same. When we did our last album, it was close to fucking fist-fighting.

I wrote that fucking tune, play it the way I wrote it else we ain't fucking doing it.
I'm gonna do it like this.
No you're fucking not. Play it this way.

And that's how I try and get the best out of him. It might not look like that, but it's what I'm doing.

So, I was back in Broken Bones. Now there was just the small matter of winkling out the new bass player who'd been recruited to the band while I was gone. But he got the hoof fairly quickly. Mind you, he went on to join Conflict, so it all worked out well enough for him. We get on now, although it's fair to say it took a while...

The next thing I did was quit drinking. No drink, no drugs. I cleaned up for about a year. Since the spell in hospital I'd started putting weight on, so I stopped drinking, stopped the drugs, and started exercising. A keep-fit binge. Weights and stuff.

I didn't join a gym, I just worked out at home. I wasn't doing an impression of *Rocky* running up and down the steps of Stoke town hall, nothing like that. I just did things my way, and got myself clean. It helped. I was sharper, fitter, my weight came down.

Things were looking good, again.

bones

Tezz?

I've never had a clue what he's going to do.

And nor has he.

FOAD

On the abortive tour of the US with the Subs, the one where I made it as far as Toronto, we'd been touring with the Exploited. Now their guitarist, Karl Morris – whose path would cross with mine many times over the years – had had a big fall-out with Wattie, and left the band, so I thought I'd invite him to be the second guitar player with Broken Bones. Together, we did the *Fuck Off And Die* album. I was on bass, Bones played guitar, Carl was second guitar, Baz played drums, and Nobby did the vocals.

It was a great album. It still is. We toured it, sporadically. And then we had a fall-out ourselves, and Karl got pushed out. It was money issues, as these things so often are, but it wasn't down to me. Someone else in the band was unhappy about the cash getting split five ways instead of four. So, the usual happened. There was bitching and moaning, and eventually Karl left. Then we did a mini-album called *Trader In Death*, without him.

It wasn't as good a sound, partly because we're missing that second guitar, but also because of the production. *Fuck Off And Die* is the best-produced album we ever did, because I insisted there were no pedals used. There would be no saturation of sound, just an amplifier and a guitar. Pure, clean, and simple. That was how it had to be. And it turned out the best. Plus I had Karl's backing, which was partly why I brought him in, knowing that Bones would follow suit and fall in line.

With Karl gone, we were back to being a four piece. And then we lost Nobby, the singer. He wanted out of Stoke-on-Trent, like every fucker else, and he met a woman, saw his chance, and took it. She lived in New York, so he moved there too, to be with her. He's still there now, although he's not with the same woman. He didn't carry on in music, mind, but then he couldn't shake a tambourine if his life depended on it, and all the times I've been in NYC I've never seen him. I've been there with bands, I've even heard he's been in the same venue, but I've never even clapped eyes on him.

So when he left to go to NYC, and since I'd lost all the weight and was feeling good about myself, and we needed a front man, I thought *Fuck it, I'll do it*. I didn't want to play bass at the same time, though, so I got someone in who I knew could do it. Broken Bones became a four piece with me on vocals and a young kid called Darren on bass. It was all right. It was adequate. Nothing more.

Being the singer after playing the bass felt like a lot of hard work. It was weird. You've nothing in your hands, for starters. If someone had offered me a straight choice between being at the front or playing bass, I'd have chosen playing bass every time, no question. But Nobby had gone and there was no-one to fill his boots, so... *I'll fucking do it.* I've seen some videos of it. It doesn't look bad. Didn't sound bad. So it was all right. But in comparison with playing bass, this was work.

I was still the front man when I went to the States again, on a two-and-a-half month tour.

Broken Bones, with the Subs. Now you might think that – seeing as the last time I'd seen them had been after the incident with the turd in Toronto – spending two-and-a-half months on the road with them would be awkward. It wasn't at all.

Firstly, that was because there were never any problems between me and Charlie. He looks after himself, and whatever happens in the band, as far as he's concerned it happens and then it figures itself out. No-one's going to fuck with his position, so he saw Toronto as history, which didn't concern him.
Secondly, we had a new tour manager, a guy named Rab, who had been the Subs drummer at some point, and was a mad Scots guy who could find a fight on an empty desert island. If I'd ever thought for a moment about wrapping a turd round his head, knowing that would have helped me decide against it. And I do tend to try and learn from my mistakes. The severe ones, anyway.

Deptford wasn't there either – he might have been with the Exploited. Steve Roberts, who was totally drunk all the time, was on drums. The others were just fill-ins. The tour itself was two-and-a-half months spent criss-crossing America in vans. None of your REM tour bus comfort and luxury. This was pure graft. I think we had a motorhome, like a big RV, and we were all in it. Us and the Subs, with the backline in a trailer and a couple of Canadian roadies who worked for both bands. One tech, and a sound engineer who did all the driving and worked the gigs. All of us earned our corn.

Graft or no graft, it was a really good tour. We covered a lot of places, as you can imagine. Sometimes the Subs headlined, sometimes we did. That was up to the venues. The LA gig was in an open-air bowl, and the kids tore up the barricade and everything, fighting with security. I've seen a video of that gig, and I'm at the front of the stage, and in front of me there's just this line of guys in bright orange jackets. Security. Dozens of them. But then it did get a bit nutty. We blew the Subs away that day, mind. Which meant Charlie would get on stage next day determined to up the ante and blow *us* away. There was a friendly rivalry, which was good seeing as we were on the same bus. Swings and roundabouts. One day, we were better. Another, it was them. When you're on tour, it's your life, it's what you're here for. It's your job, your dreams, your everything. So a good tour is something to savour.

I couldn't do what normal people do, get up every day and go to a job they hate. It's punishing. I see people do it, and come home of an evening and get stuck into the bottle, and it's horrible.

This was a great tour, but that doesn't mean there weren't some shit gigs too. In Portland, Oregon, I did a back flip off a humungous high stage, expecting the crowd to catch me, and every fucker moved. The crowd parted like the Red Sea, and I landed, bang! *Oops*, I thought. *Not doing that again.* I'm surprised I didn't break anything, but – as the incident with the balcony in Deptford had made clear – I do have a knack for coming off high things and not breaking anything.

Perhaps it's because I got into karate when I was a kid. Maybe if there's one thing that taught me, it helped me learn to land.

I'd had my year of not drinking and getting fit while I was in Stoke, but out on the road, that was never going to last. Not drinking while everyone else is having whatever they want? Just sitting there, watching? No chance. Fucking impossible. I mean I do it now, but back then? Not a hope. I might have reined it in a little, but I was still a northern nutter. I was certainly no saint.

I wasn't as mental as I had been on the Subs turd-in-Toronto tour, but I was still fairly wild. However much I reined it in, there was a lot of fighting. Almost all of it with skinheads. They've a tendency to really piss me off, and we had a few run-ins with them. For the most part, we came out on top. Not always, mind you, but for the most part.

I was in a good place. In comparison with the Subs tour where I'd got sacked, life was much, much better. I was on a mission. I'd had a year of exercise and not drinking which had helped me get a focus, I was out on the road with a band, doing vocals in Broken Bones, touring – which I loved above anything – and the tour had been good. Two and-a-half months of good gigs, fun, and partying. And there'd been plenty of fighting, too. All was well.

Then the tour came to an end, as all things do, and I decided not to go home.

I started a new life, instead. In the States.

Chicago

The end of the tour came, and I stayed in Chicago. I'd been looking for a reason to make a fresh start somewhere new, and during the tour I met this girl. Christine, from Chicago. She ticked all the boxes of what I wanted, she was the girl I felt most comfortable with, she came with us on the tour for a week – till we played Canada, and she had to go home – and in that time the decision was made. I was going to start a new life, in Chicago.

It could have been anywhere, this new life. It wasn't that I was particularly sold on Chicago itself. But Christine happened to live there, so that's where I was going, too. I told the band, and they didn't care. I told them I was staying in the States, and that was it.

You can go on without me. That OK, Bones?
Yeah.

And they carried on without me, and that was fine. Wherever it was that they flew back from at the end of the tour, I can't remember, but I got dropped off in Chicago, and it was goodbye to them, and hello new life. It was the end of summer. The weather was great. I was living with Christine, in her flat in gaytown, just walking distance from the baseball stadium at Wrigley Field. There was a lake. There was a beach. This place had everything, and all of it was good. All I could think was

This. Is. Beautiful.

And it was. But I hadn't come across winter there yet. That's fucking harsh. I'd learn about that soon enough, but for now it's summer.

Christine works in the local punk-metal store, and is involved with merchandise and design, and I'm wandering around Chicago, hanging around at the lake, and the beach, and in the evening we head out to the bars and she introduces me to the punks and the skinheads on the scene. They're cool guys, and they do two things: they adopt me, and they get me a job.

The job is cash in hand. Black economy. It has to be, because at this point – as far as the US government and the IRS are concerned – I'm an illegal. I've only just landed in Chicago, and I've no papers or anything. So cash in hand work is all I can do. But that's fine. I'm working at the same place as a lot of the other guys on the scene. A club called Medusa's, down on Clarke and School.

During the day I'm helping build sculptures and paint the place – because Medusa's is a gay bar and has a different theme each weekend, so there's always stuff to build and paint – which is steady work, gentle and relaxing. And at night I'm on the door and working security, which isn't.

You see, as well as being a gay bar, Medusa's is a juice bar. It doesn't serve any alcohol. You might think that would make life easy, that doing security there would be a piece of piss. You'd be wrong. Everyone turned up pissed anyway, because they'd been drinking elsewhere. And it stayed open till 4.30 in the morning, so everyone turned up.

There'd be regular customers. Then there'd be gang members. And – of course – Medusa's was a gay club, so at some point during the night you'd have guys wanting to fuck each other

No! You can't do that here, lads!

On top of all of that, you'd get the Marines. Out of their fucking minds and just wanting to fight. Everywhere else was shut, and they'd all pile in to Medusa's, pissed, and ready to rumble. And the thing about Marines, is they don't come in ones or twos, they come in platoons. So these could be long, long nights, especially as there were just eight of us patrolling over the four floors of the club, none of us armed with anything more sturdy than a plastic flashlight.

If it came to a ruck with the Marines, we'd all pile in, because we had to. But we were strictly forbidden from being tooled up. A lot of the time, that didn't work out too well. Plastic flashlights are worth fuck all, when push comes to shove, but we weren't allowed anything metal, or anything with a bit of weight to it. It was like going to a gunfight with a catapult. But the guys who ran the club were all gay and they didn't want any violence.

Or at least, any violence from us.

These flashlights are useless.
Don't they work, Tezz?
Yeah. Till you hit someone. Then they just break.
Er, you really shouldn't be hitting our customers.
I shouldn't?
No.

Do you know who's coming to your club??
Well...
Marines.
They're not that bad...
Hordes of marines.
But...
Hordes of drunken marines.
You see...
Hordes of drunken marines, and they want to kill each other, and they want to kill us.
We don't want violence, Tezz.
Is there any chance of a javelin? Maybe a tank?
Hmmm. Have you tried talking your way out of the trouble?

So every night was a free-for-all, because the Marines were pissed and knew all we could take them on with was bad language and a plastic flashlight. Unfortunately for me, I'd be pissed as well, so my response was always *Yeah. Bring it on.*

And they did. There was all these stairs in the club, and there'd be people flying down the stairs every night. Every single night. Most times it was Marines. Sometimes it was me.

I was living in Chicago, finding my feet, then spending every night getting knocked off them.

Social Life

I'm in Chicago. I've got a job, cash in hand. I've got money in my pocket. It's a good start, but it's not enough. I know I can't keep being an illegal, and I can't keep fighting Marines. That means things need to change.

First off, I married Christine. I hadn't been in Chicago long when that happened, because it had always been the intention. I had nothing to hide. I'd laid my cards out on the table back when we'd met while Broken Bones were touring with the Subs.

I'll come with you, we'll get married, I'll get my green card. Whatever happens after that happens.

And she agreed, because she was smitten. Back in the day, I wasn't bad looking. I had all the right patter, and there weren't so many miles on the clock. So I asked, she said yes, we did the deed, and – bingo! – I'm now able to work legitimately in the US. But like I say, I don't really want to spend my working hours clocking in just so I can clock out Marines, so I move more into helping build and create the art that went up in Medusa's each week.

Myself and this guy Chris Forney – who was one of my best friends, but who's dead now, like so many of them are – we really got into making the art. We'd make these humungous sculptures for a fella called Tom Hemingway. He'd come in, say

This week, I think we should have...I dunno... Easter Island heads round the club. How's that

sound? Yeah... Easter Island heads. Can you do that, guys?

And we'd crack on with the carving, the painting, the putting all the stuff together. Tom knew he could leave us to get on with it, and trust us to get it done. Me and Chris would have a laugh doing it, and it beat the living daylights out of doing security. Why put myself and my body on the line when wielding a paintbrush puts cash in my pocket? It's a no-brainer. Mind you, I was quickly learning that however fast I painted to earn the money, Christine would be spending it on treadmills and weights and god knows what. The house was like a fucking gym.

So money was always tight. Life was a little bit hand-to-mouth, but with fewer fists involved than when I was fighting Marines. I've got my green card, I'm legal, I'm in a pretty good place. I'm working at Medusa's – I worked there for four years all told – and that suits me down to the ground. If other things come along, I know I can go off and do them, and then come back to Medusa's, because Tom will always want me to build some strange sculpture or other, and Chris will be happy to see me. Everything is set up just how I want it. If I want to, I can find myself a band, head off in a van, play some gigs, make my music, and when I come back to Chicago and Christine I can pick up where I left off, at Medusa's.

Perfect.
But I had no band. That wasn't so good.
And that needed to change.

I'm keeping my eyes open, putting the word out, doing little auditions here and there. Every now and then I'll jam with a band, just to keep my hand in. I fly to New York and audition as singer with a band called School Of Violence, a hardcore band whose work I know, but I don't get it, and I fly back to Chicago. It may seem crazy to go all that distance just because there was the possibility of being singer – not even playing guitar – in a band, but moving to the States had never been just about moving to the States. It was about moving to the States and doing music. It had to be, I didn't know how to do anything else.

Doing music, though, is taking time to happen. But my social life is taking off, and that will lay the foundations for all the things – good and bad – that happen later. I've already got a taste for drink, drugs, and adventure, and I'm naturally drawn to people who look like they're going to provide two or more of the three. Even if – or maybe especially when – these are people that everyone else is urging me to keep well clear of.

Why don't they like them? What is it?
By the time I'd find out, it was usually too late.

Chris Forney, who I did the sculptures with, was one of those people. Medusa's would let him in the club during the day, to work on the art, but they wouldn't dream of letting him in the place at night. They'd known him long before I arrived on the scene, and he had a reputation. He was drunk all the time. Usually on drugs. Always fighting. A proper loose cannon.

Don't mix with him, Tezz!

So of course, I didn't listen. This was a man whose dad had bought him a car, and Chris had crashed it while he was off his face, trashed it, and walked away.

Drink? *Tick.*
Drugs? *Tick.*
Adventure? *Tick.*

What wasn't to like?

At some point in my time in Chicago, Chris got an apartment next to mine, and – typically – his bathroom was broken so we had to share the one bathroom between us. One night Chris got home drunk and couldn't find his keys. He'd locked himself out of his apartment. So he fell into the bathroom and slept in the bath. And while he was asleep, passed out drunk, he kicked through the wall. Just kicked it through.

I liked that. I liked *him*. With Chris around, life was never dull. That meant a lot of people – people who were generally a good deal more sensible than me – would keep a wide berth from him, but it drew me in.

Adventure, right? Who can say *no* to adventure? Chris couldn't. Heroin took him, the adventures ended, and he was gone.

My other good mate was Joe Kelly. A short, compact Irish kid a bit younger than me. Like Chris, I met him through the guys at Medusa's. He wasn't working there though, because the owners didn't care for him. He was a bit too opinionated, I think, a little bit too gobby. And a little bit nutty. He'd fight, if he had to – not that I ever saw it – and he always had a beer, always had drugs on hand. The two of us hit it off, and all through my time in Chicago, Joe was someone who helped me out when I needed it, put opportunities my way when that was something he could do.

You see, I was always drawn towards the people that the Americans didn't like. Maybe that's down to the difference between the two cultures. Brits look at Americans and shake their heads, and Americans look at Brits and don't understand us either. I don't know. It could be that, or it could just be me. Either way, I was somewhere new and I was absorbing everything, and Joe saw something in me and I saw something in him. I still don't know what it is, but we were good mates, and of all the people I met in Chicago, Joe's the funniest, the one who entertained me most, the one who went out of his way to dig me out of whatever hole I'd thrown myself into.

But that's all in the future. For now, I'm drinking, and jamming in bands, and working at Medusa's. It's all good. And then I end up in the background of a video for a band, part of the crowd. Some band are shooting the video for their song in Medusa's, and all the guys who work there, and all their mates, we're all in the video. We get to drink beer all day, and all we have to do for the video is look like a bunch of goons, which is what we do best.

I don't know who the band are, and they've no idea who I am, but the video is for a track called *Stigmata*.

The band is called Ministry.

And our paths will cross again.

Ministry

Time ticks on. I'm jamming with some bands, and playing in others. I'm in a local Chicago band, 77 Luscious Babes – god knows where the name came from, but I just play guitar and it's not for me to question – with some mates, and we have a few releases. Well, one release. On top of that I do quite a few more band auditions in New York, turning up and hoping to get signed, and going home with nothing. One time I was there, and there was another band called Pearl Jam. No-one had heard of them, they were just like us, out for a label. Next thing you know, they're signed. Then they're humungous. Us? We're still looking for a label. That's how it goes. That's what happens.

So things are steady. But, even with Chris and his special kind of chaos, life's a little dull. Then I get a call from Joe.

Tezz, that you?
Yeah.
Fancy a beer?
You bet.
Good. I've something you may be interested in.
Really?
Yeah. I think you'll like it.

I meet Joe in a bar, and he tells me his news. Ministry are going out on tour, and they need a guitarist. The band is Jorgensen's baby, and he does all the work in the studio, but for live gigs, they need someone there, so there's an opening for the right person. Joe's going to be doing the tour, which is how he knows about it, and he's giving me the heads up, so I can put my name down for an audition. *Here*, he says, giving me a CD. *This is what you'll need to learn.* I put the CD in my pocket, we chew the fat and have a few beers, and eventually I make my way home. Next morning – or next afternoon – I get up, stick the CD in the stereo, and listen. Bloody hell.

From the very first moment I heard the tunes I was hooked. I listened to *Burning Inside* and went

Whoah! What's this??!! This is great!!!

It was aggressive – I'd heard some other stuff of theirs which was more like The Cure, which wasn't my bag at all – and a bit odd, which meant I took to it right away because I'd been playing that kind of thing for years. So finding a guitar line was easy. I practised the songs, went along to the audition, did my thing, and that was it. I was in, straight off. I'd been in the States just over a year, and now I'd got a gig with Ministry. This was big.

The first gig I did with them was off in Wisconsin somewhere, I think. Milwaukee, maybe. I'm not sure. But then we came back to Chicago and played the Aragon Ballroom. The band's hometown gig, and it's sold out, sold out solid every night. It was amazing. I'd never been in anything like it.

Jorgensen had gone out of his way to find everything that he wanted, and everything to do with the tour was top notch. No expense was spared. PA, lights, the stage set that created this industrial look he wanted – there were wire frames at the front of the stage which people climbed on during the gig before diving back into the crowd, or getting kicked off by the band – all of it was exactly how Jorgensen wanted it. Ministry were taking off right now, and whatever he wanted, he got.

Part of what he wanted was British people in the band. I was on guitar, Martin Atkins out of Public Image was on drums, and there was some Scottish guy doing one of the vocals. I say *one* because there were three or even four vocalists on the live shows, an absolute collage of vocals.

There was the Scottish guy. Jello Biafra was doing Lard and spoken word. Nivic Ogre from Skinny Puppy was doing whatever he did. And Joe Kelly was another vocalist, doing the vocals Iain Mackay from Minor Threat had done in the studio. He wouldn't show for the tour, so Joe was stepping in, just like I'd stepped in on guitar. Each of us seeing the opportunity and diving in there.

This was a humungous production. It wasn't four guys – bass, two guitars, and drums – getting up on stage and doing the usual. This was something else. Lots of people, professional crew, PA, lights, stage set, the lot. We even had our own camera crew, filming the gig every day. How much did all that cost? I've no idea. It's not my concern. I was just a hired gun, I knew that, but – like everyone else – I'm getting outrageously paid, so it's a good time. I also knew I'd landed properly on my feet with this, getting such a good gig so soon after starting my new life in a new country, but I knew – equally and without a shadow of a doubt – that it was going to be short-lived, because that's how my life is. You get a good time, but you can't hold onto it, and who knows what's next? Maybe it'll get better... and maybe it won't. With any luck, and with enough time, it'll pick up at some other point down the road. But unfortunately, those really good times, the rich pickings like Ministry, they're few and far between. You've just got to enjoy them while they're there.

We did the gigs at the Aragon, and we were off. Away on this massive tour. A proper tour with tour buses and hotels. None of your grafting it across the country in a clapped-out van for months on end, playing small venues, and just getting by. This was proper. This was what I'd had a glimpse of when REM got me back out of Canada. This was how it should be done. We did that tour, came back to Chicago to catch our breath, and went off on another. Everything was looking good, incredibly good. And then the cracks started to show.

You see, that tour was the one that made Ministry huge. Now everyone wanted a piece of them, and everyone wanted a piece of Jorgensen. But people fuck up. He fucked up. I fucked up. That's what happens. That's what people do. You get it all, for a moment, but you can't have it for more than that moment. I know that. With the best will in the world, you can't hold on to it. And the partying doesn't help.

I would always play the gigs straight. Sober. But after the gig, I'd party. Boy, I'd party. However much anybody else wanted to party, I'd take it to a different level. A lot of them couldn't deal with it. The bus ended up being segregated.

This is the band bus. The crew and the camera guys and whoever else were on different buses, and I can't speak about what happened there. But I can tell you without a shadow of a doubt that our bus was segregated. You had part of the band, the bass player and the drummers, the book-reading nancy boys down the front, sipping cups of tea, doing yoga and checking their chakras are aligned, and then you'd have the nutters in the back lounge. And that was us. We'd have women back there with us, of course. Everyone's off their tits, and anything goes. We're modern-day barbarians, pillaging our way across the land, and it's nuts, fucking nuts.

Looking back, it's horrible.

I'm not stupid. I know I'm treading on toes. I'm getting thumbs up from my part of the band, and thumbs down from the other part. As far as I'm concerned, they don't count. Jorgensen, he's loving it. Because he loves stoking the fire, and then putting the blame on someone else when it all gets out of hand. When it goes wrong, I'm the scapegoat – *It wasn't me, it was him!* – but he's there in the back lounge partying with us. It's him, me, Mike Scaccia, all the rebels. One of the guys – Jorgensen's mate who played bass on the live shows, who wasn't even plugged in, but just wanted to be part of the whole rock'n'roll circus – he killed himself after the tour. OD'd on drugs. What's that tell you about how we were behaving? The Scottish singer, he put a book out later, and slated me and Scaccia. Said something about me being *like a Neanderthal bricklayer*.

I can tell you now, that's bullshit. I've never touched a brick in my life.

We do the tour, three months or whatever, and I go back to Chicago. I've had a blast. I've played guitar and I've partied like you wouldn't believe. I'm getting on well with Jorgensen, because he's a megalomaniac and he likes me. I'm in a pretty good place, I think. I've got my green card, I'm legal, I've just been on tour with this very well-paid job playing guitar in Ministry.
OK, so now I'm back in Chicago and back to Christine, and I know I'm already on thin ice there. Nothing ever lasts. We're a couple of years in to our relationship, and I'm a monster. Still, things can only get better. That's what I tell myself. Things can only get better.

Why wouldn't they?
I'm out in the States, and I'm living the dream.

nigel again

Tezz overall? He's a complex character. I've seen quiet Tezz, a reflective Tezz, and – back when I was in the band – a shy Tezz. If my girlfriend came along to rehearsals, it was clear Tezz didn't know how to handle himself round a girl, at all. He'd come over like some Johnny Rotten character, trying to shock or whatever. He changed from when it was just us guys together.

Above all, though, he's immensely determined. After Discharge signed to Clay, Tezz disappeared. We didn't see him for three or four months. He'd hidden himself away in his room, and taught himself guitar. He was that driven. He came back in the shop, and he could play guitar. When Acker left Discharge, he taught himself drums. I've never met anyone who's a more natural musician than Tezz. He's just got it. He puts his mind to it, works at it, teaches himself. Guitar. Drums. Bass.

If you want a story that shows his willpower, try this. Tezz got quite podgy one time. He disappeared for two months, came back in and he was three stone lighter. I asked him

How the hell did you do that?
I never eat anything after five o'clock.

He made it sound easy. He's got that discipline. He's living the dream and being exactly what he wants to be.

And how many people can say that?

Jolly Roger

It's through the tour with Ministry that I pick up some more work. It's not making music, but – for a musician – it's probably the next best thing. It's working in the industry. I come back to Chicago, and I start working for Jam Productions, on the local crew for gigs.

It's good money. $18 an hour for turning up in the morning, unloading however many trucks there are, setting up the lights and the PA for the gig, doing whatever is needed, and then taking it all down at the end of the show and loading it back into the trucks. Physical graft, which I'm fine with, and a bunch of other reprobates to work with, which I'm fine with too. We'd work the gigs at the Aragon, and then walking distance away – basically across the street – was another venue, and we'd work there too. One time we did two gigs in the one night. Sex Pistols making a racket on one side of the street, Slayer on the other, and us just walking from one side of the street to the other as we were needed, throwing stuff in and out of trucks, doing the gigs. Double bubble. It doesn't get better than that.

I got the job through Jolly Roger, Ministry's tour manager. He was about ten years older than me, and he worked for Jam when he wasn't on tour, organising the crew, and making sure everything ran as it should. We'd struck up something of a friendship on the Ministry tour, because Roger was the person you turned to when you got yourself in trouble, and it doesn't take a genius to know that I've an inbuilt capacity for getting myself into that. The tour was regularly punctuated by situations – with yours truly at the heart of them – which needed Roger's special help to sort out. I think this meant he liked me. I also think he saw me as someone who needed rescuing. A lot.

He saved my arse in Colorado. After the gig, a girl accused me of molesting her, and went to the police. They came looking for me, but as they climbed on the front of one bus to search it, I slipped off by the back door and got on another. We had three buses. I skipped from bus to bus to bus, having a drink and a chat in each one before scooting out the back as the cops arrived. There was every chance the game – and as far as I was concerned, this was a game – would go on all night. Then I heard over the driver's intercom that the cops had had enough. They were getting pissed off. Wiser heads than mine suggested this wouldn't help me or anyone else, and it was time I turned myself in. So I did.

Five minutes later I'm in cuffs in the back of a police car. I could be going to jail for something I may or may not have done. But that's not what's worrying me. I've just remembered that a few hours earlier I scored myself a bunch of drugs from a random stranger, which was how my life worked at the time.

Hi. What have you got?
Er...this.
OK. I'll have three.

In this particular case, this means I'm sitting in a police car with a sheet of acid in the pocket of my jeans.

That's a big offence. If the cops find that, it won't be good. Not in any way, shape, or form. I'm looking at some serious time behind bars. Then Jolly Roger comes to my rescue. I don't know what he does or what he says, but he's got the gift of the gab and a very persuasive manner. Next thing I know I'm out of the car and out of the cuffs. The police are going to run us out of town instead.

Well, Roger, we'll let this fella go.
Thank you, officer.
He's a lucky man.
He is, officer. I'll make sure he knows.
And you'll forget about your hotels.
Yes, officer.
You won't be staying here.
No, officer, we won't.
You just get in your vehicles and get out of town.
We will, officer.
Right now.
Thank you. We're gone. Tezz, come with me.

The police put cars front and rear of Ministry's whole entourage, turned on the blues and twos, and escorted the buses and me and my jeans with that big sheet of acid all the way out of town, and out of Colorado.

Thank you, officers. And I really mean that.

I owed Jolly Roger for that, big style. I knew he was good at organising people, and making sure the crew were up to the mark, but now I saw he could deal with coppers too. He was an all-rounder. A legend. A big man, an American Indian who was a humungous size and had a character to match. He had to be a big character to keep us all in line. But that was what he was good at. Verbally, he'd let you know what was what, but he wouldn't ever put his hands on you. He wouldn't have to. He'd just take you down verbally. And he had a code. Thoro was respect involved.

If he could trust you, you were in.
If you crossed him, that was it. Out.

He helped people out of the shit, too. Mainly, as I say, that meant me. He didn't have to do it, but – luckily – when I was in trouble, he was there and he never seemed to hold it against me. He got me out of the back of a police car with the power of his words, and he saved me from getting my head kicked in when we were in LA, too.

We were doing a gig, and Jorgensen's got the American flag and he's waving it around. No problem. Then, somehow, it's on fire. Problem. How this happened, I don't know. Whether Jorgensen did it, or someone else did it, or god himself reached down with a box of matches and a cheeky grin, I haven't a clue. But I know it wasn't me.

I'm sure of that. Because if it had been me, that would have come out in the wash at some point, and it hasn't. At the time, though, those considerations are more or less irrelevant, because security are going fucking mental at seeing the stars and stripes in flames. Anyone who isn't American (because what good American would set fire to their own flag, right?) is right in the line of fire. And I'm the poor sap who they've got in their sights. Partly that's because they don't like my attitude, and partly it's because I'm near enough to the incident to be put in the frame for setting the flag on fire in the first place.

This isn't a career-changing incident, it's a life changer. There's a chopping block, and my head's on it.

I knew I was in trouble when this humungous guy on the security, this fella who was eight feet tall and just as wide, walked up to me, poked me in the chest and went

No, you fucking don't.

There was no way I was going to get away with fighting this fella. I knew that with every fibre of my body. When he said something, you either got on your way or you did what he said, and right now neither of those options were on offer. He was just going to kill me. And then his mates were going to do it again.

Then Roger stepped in. He was very forceful. Powerful, but not provocative. The kind of guy you listened to. He had a lifetime of dealing with situations like this, years of experience in smoothing ruffled feathers and pouring oil on troubled waters. However ridiculous an outrage, you'd never see him take the piss or lose his temper, and things almost always ended up with handshakes all round as Roger found a way of calming things down and sorting them out without bloodshed. At least, he'd always managed it so far.

I hoped he'd do it again. Luckily for me, he did.

He'd saved my bacon twice now. And given me a job. I'm sitting pretty. I've got my green card. I'm playing guitar with Ministry. I've got money in my pocket, and a great job on the crew with Jam. On top of that, Jolly Roger's got my back. Life is just about perfect.

And then it all goes wrong.

Fall

My fall from grace came hard and fast.

I'd got my green card by marrying Christine, and that stopped me being an illegal. It didn't mean I started playing by the rules. Back then, that just wasn't in my nature. Yes, being legal meant I could go on tour with Ministry, but when it came to paying taxes.... That was something else entirely. They sent me some forms, and I just stuck them in the bin.

You see, that was my attitude. I wasn't going to think about things, I wasn't going to weigh things up and work out what course of action made most sense, I'd just do what I wanted. If I fancied hopping from bus to bus to avoid the cops, I would. If I didn't want to pay taxes, I wouldn't. And if I was away from home, and there was drink, and drugs, and women... Well, who was I to say no?

It was only a matter of time till Christine had enough. OK, so it wasn't as if I had to worry about someone taking a photo on a smartphone or spilling their guts on social media, but that wasn't going to save my skin. A little while after I came back to Chicago, she decided she didn't want me anywhere near her, and moved to LA.

This wasn't good. It left me to my own devices, and - as we already know - they ran to women, drink, and drugs. Before I knew it, I was doing way too much cocaine. Way, way too much cocaine. The girl I started seeing got me into that. Not that I'm putting the blame on her - it was my choice to take the stuff – but she was involved with me getting access to the drugs so easily, because she was part of a gang dealing drugs. In a matter of weeks, I was drowning in a sea of cocaine.

Of course, I'm coked out of my head, and think everything's great. But it isn't. My job with Jam goes, because I start blowing gigs off, saying I'll turn up and not turning up, and before long Jolly Roger stops asking me, stops phoning to offer me work. He never sacked me, never said *You can't work any more*, but he's not a stupid man. He knew what I was doing. He knew everyone on the Jam crew was a fuck-up, and he'd taken us in and given us a chance, but he's far too smart to go chasing after someone who's spending every waking minute doing coke.

But I don't care, because I'm full of coke. My wife's gone? Let's do some coke. My job's gone? Let's do some coke. Because that's what I do now.

I marry the girl who's scoring the coke for me, and I do more coke. Then one night it all goes tits up. I come home and she's in bed with a bunch of guys. Next thing I know they're on me, kicking me, punching me. They run me out of my own house, and all of a sudden I'm in Medusa's, sleeping on the floor, trying to work out what happened and how I got there. The break-up with Christine kind of kicked it all off, I know that, and now everything I had is gone. Her. My job. My home. A few months ago I was touring the States with Ministry. Now I'm living at Medusa's, doing precious little but drink and take cocaine.

It's a proper come-down. Then when you think things can't get worse, I get stabbed. Me and Chris Forney go out to a mexican restaurant, and fucking skinheads – who are out to get me because of past misdemeanours – come in and it all kicks off. I get stabbed in the back and they plant a fork in my head. And my nose gets broken. Again. I didn't have to go to hospital, but they opened me up. It wasn't a good day, but then no day where you get a fork in the head and have to bed down in a nightclub is ever going to count as good, is it?

Who knows how long I'd have been at Medusa's or what would have happened if it hadn't been for Joe. My mate Joe Kelly watching over me, looking out for me again, just like he did when he got me the Ministry gig in the first place. He's got friends, and he knows what's going on. Word reaches him that I'm on the skids and living in Medusa's, and he pulls me out of the shit. Next thing I know, he's got me out of the city and in a place Jorgensen owns, which he lets Mike Scaccia use. Joe puts me in there, and tells me

Stay here. Stay here until the dust settles.

Because by now my life's a proper mess. A drug gang's out to get me. Skinheads are out to get me. I'm a drinker who's spending his days chock full of coke, and when I go into the bars in town people are telling me to get out. Because I'm bad news. I'm a liability. For my own good, Joe knows I need to go away, lock myself away from all my old haunts and sort myself out.

Joe pulled my nuts out of the fire, because he knew I wasn't capable of doing it for myself. And being the fool that I am, I never thanked him for it. I didn't even recognise what he'd done for me.

And when the chance to tour with Ministry came round again, I took it.

Frying Pan

Joe's got me out of the city, away from the skinheads and the drugs, and we're still mates. Hiding me safely away in Scaccia's house has given me a chance to get my act together and clean up, but I'm still skint, so when he tells me Ministry are going to be doing the Lollapolooza tour in the summer of '92, I grab it with both hands.

This is a massive tour. Thirty-six festival dates all across North America through the summer of 1992, with Ministry on the main stage just before the Red Hot Chili Peppers, who are headlining.

Before us, there's Soundgarden, Ice Cube, The Jesus and Mary Chain, Pearl Jam – who are doing all right for themselves since I met them at that audition in New York – and Lush. And that's just the main stage. There's a load of bands on other stages, too.

Anyone who's significant at the time, they're on this tour. It's going to be immense. It's going to be a lot of fun. And by the time it all finishes – with a three-day run in Irvine, California – in September, I should have managed to put together enough money to set me back up on my feet.

That was the plan, anyway. In so far as I had a plan. It was simple enough: play music, have fun, save money. And it might just have worked, but for one small problem.

Early on in the tour, temptation crossed my path.

We're a few dates in, and I meet a girl. She's oriental, she's very good-looking, and she's completely off her tits, because she has a BIG bag of drugs. Speed. Crystal meth. She waves it around and all I can think is

Fucking hell! Look at that!!

and any plans for the future went right out of the window, right then. I wanted those drugs. I needed those drugs. I knew nothing else mattered. I also knew they'd cost me an arm and a leg, though, and I needed to do something about that. Fortunately, I'm a sneaky little fucker. I took her bag, and hid it.

The instant she realised the bag had gone, she panicked. She was out of her mind on meth already, but now she was out of her mind on fear as well. *Ohmygodwheresthefuckingbag!!* And this was where my sneakiness really paid off. Her bag's gone? Shit, that's a disaster. Does she want me to help her look for it? I'd be happy to, of course. Who wouldn't help a friend in their hour of need? I'm so sincere, I almost convince myself, but it's all about waiting for the moment where she promises me that if I find the missing bag, she'll give me half. As soon as she said that I was like

Oh. What's this? Is this it? Look! I've found it.

She's so happy to have the bag back she doesn't think to wonder what just went on, and wham bam thank you ma'am, I've got half of a big bag of drugs. I'm beyond pleased with myself.

As far as I'm concerned, right now I'm the smartest man on the planet. And on one level – the scoring lots of drugs without paying for them level – yes, I am. On another level – which involves sorting myself out and getting back on my feet – what I'm doing is way beyond stupid. A few months ago I was full of coke. Now I'm going to be just as full of crystal meth, and given the quantity of drugs available to me already, that's completely unnecessary. And unlikely to end well.

You see, there'd already been the incident with the mushrooms.

We were playing one of the dates up north, near Chicago. A mate, a really good tattooist I knew, was at the gig. *Here, Tezz,* he said. *Have a mushroom, for later.* And I thought

Later??

So I munched it. Not my brightest move. By the time we were supposed to be playing, I was completely off my tits. I was *seeing* noise, seeing it as shapes and colours, feeling every single sound with every cell in my body. It was too much. It was unbearable. I knew that any moment now the others were going to come looking for me to get ready to go on stage, and here I was, with eyes like saucers, not knowing which way was up or what I was looking at. There was just one thing I was sure of: the gig was fucked.

So I did the only thing it was possible to do.
I hid.

I crawled underneath the drum riser, curled up in a ball, and hid with with my fingers in my ears while the rest of Ministry played. It's the only gig I've ever bailed on in my life. I stayed there for the whole set. When the gig finished, I crawled out from under the drum riser, and everyone was firing questions at me, all of which boiled down to one thing.

Where the fuck were you, Tezz?

I couldn't answer them. I couldn't even talk. Joe took one look at me and he knew I was off my tits, but it didn't take a genius to work that out. Jorgensen, he knew too. He didn't care. I wasn't going to get paid for the gig – we all knew that – but hey, that was fair enough, you know.

Somehow, for some reason I can't quite put my finger on, being in Ministry's not as much fun this time round. The band are different. There's a displacement between me and some of the other members. A tension. Something bordering on hatred, maybe. What I've done to deserve it, I don't know. Somewhere, at some point – and I can't really be sure when or where, but I think it may have been Louisiana, that french part of the States – someone knocked me out with a bottle. I was blind drunk, I came out of a party, I was standing on the street, and someone came up behind me and hit me over the head with a bottle.

It could have been a random stranger. It might have been someone at the party. It's possible it was a member of the band, or even god himself.

I don't know. All I know is one of the crew takes me to hospital, gets me stitched up, and I come back and carry on exactly the same as I was before.

I'm partying harder than ever. I've got a big bag of crystal meth, and I'm working my way through it. I'm not sleeping. For what feels like weeks, I'm drinking and taking meth and inhabiting a world where getting hit over the head with a bottle is par for the course and nothing to worry about.

I'm invulnerable.
Immortal.
I don't need to sleep.

And then, I reach tipping point, and it all just falls apart.

Fireworks

We've got to Texas. And we're all out of control. Every night we're going hell for leather in the back lounge. It's just nuts. A blur. There's beer, tequila, drugs, and – of course – there's women. Outside, through the darkened bus windows, there's darkness. Occasional lights when we pass a vehicle on the road, or a roadhouse, or a town. But that's the real world, which is nothing to do with us. It's a million miles away. Maybe even further. Here, it's tequila, tits, and my ever-shrinking bag of crystal meth. It's my ordinary everyday madness. It's completely and utterly nuts.

Suddenly, Jorgensen produces this firework. I've never seen anything like it. It's like something you might use in big outdoor displays. Maybe that's where he got it, maybe it's something he's got his hands on from the Lollapolooza shows. I don't know. I don't care. I just know it's the biggest firework I've ever seen, and it's here – with a bunch of wasted crazies – in the back lounge of a bus in the middle of the night. The firework tube is so big you can't get your hands round it, and it's the length of your leg from your knee to the floor. That's big.

We're drunk. We're off our tits. We're a bunch of freaks who are all way way out of their gourds and we're cruising down the freeway in the middle of the night with a monster firework.

What could possibly go wrong?

Jorgensen's smoking. We're all smoking. And he takes his cigarette, and starts waving it around by the firework. *Look at this! Whaddya think of this!*

He's making out he's going to light it, but we all know he's just fucking around. And I thought *Let's call his bluff.*

I push his hand against the touch paper, and the bloody thing goes off.

Balls of fire fly out of the firework.
This thing's like a roman candle. But bigger.
Way way bigger.

I remember watching this jet of flame sail down the bus. My mouth opens in amazement. Part of me – the part that feels invulnerable because it's chock-full of crystal meth and tequila – thinks *Wow! Cool!* Another part of me knows that – in a lifetime of making decisions I may later come to regret in the cold light of day – I've just done something really really stupid. Outstandingly stupid. That part's telling me

We're going to die. We're all going to die, right here right now, and it's your fault, Tezz. It's your fault.

Because maybe it is just a tiny bit my fault that one minute we're having a party and the next we're shaking hands with death. The first ball of fire flies down the corridor of the bus, and all the curtains on the bunks catch fire. *Whoosh!* and they're gone.

Holy shit.

Everything's full of smoke. Everyone's choking, and screaming, and scrambling over each other to get the hell away from this nightmare. We've been making a racket anyway, but now the noise level goes through the roof, and the driver's wife opens the door to the front lounge to find out what's going on. She sees another ball of flame barreling down the bus toward her, and she slams the door shut before we've even had chance to scream at her to *Shut the fucking door!!* while the firework goes off again and again and again.

The bus pulls over and everyone scrambles off. We stand by the side of the freeway in the dark, not really believing what's just happened. Just glad to be alive. Then people start asking just how it is the firework went off, anyway, and pretty soon the finger's pointing at me.

I'm a fucking idiot, they tell me. I could have killed them. I'm a liability, a fucking liability who sees a humungous firework and thinks it'll be a giggle to set it off on a bus. Who has no idea of the consequences of his actions. And so on.

And I couldn't argue. Partly because I was so off my tits, but also because I was stunned. Even I knew I'd excelled myself, and not in a good way. I just had to stand there and go *Yeah. You're right.*

What else was there to say?

The driver got on the phone to the bus company. We weren't even there an hour, and another bus came, and everyone climbed on. Even me. But I'd already been told – in no uncertain terms – that this was all my fault. That there were implications. I could either pay for the damage, or I'd get dropped off the bus the moment we got to Dallas. We all knew I could never afford to pay for the damage. I'd be getting off the bus in Dallas. Whatever. Fine.

They gave me some money so I could make my way home, kicked me off the bus, and headed off into the night to play the rest of Lollapolooza.

And that was my time in Ministry done and dusted, right then.

Tezz & Bones

and their lollipops

Broken Bones

Tezz in UK Subs

Battalion Of Saints

Tezz, Micky Fitz, and a raccoon

Discharge, 2017

rock'n'roll

Discharge at Hellfest

doing what I do best

is there a better life than this?

I don't think so...

with the guitar coated in my dad's ashes

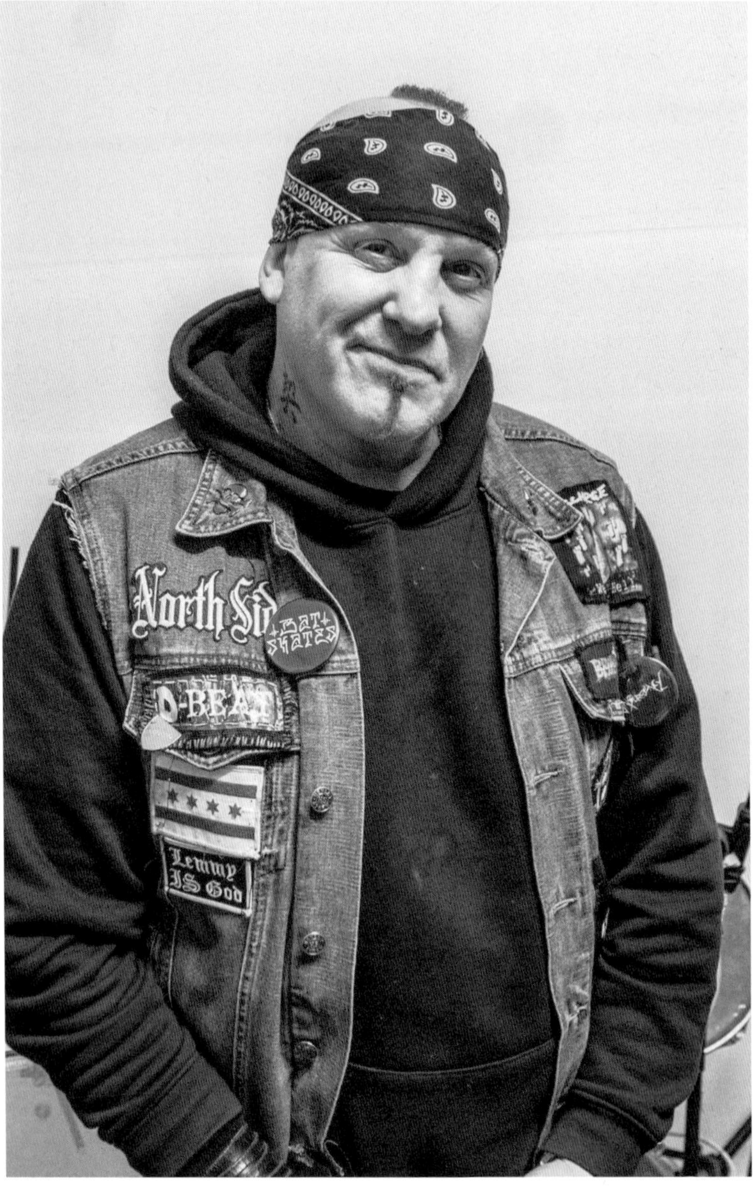
BAT SKATES
Lemmy IS God

'burbs

Years later, I see Jorgensen in Manchester, and he makes out it was him who lit the firework, and that he'd done it on purpose. I guess by then enough time had passed that he wasn't worried about the tour bus company hitting him for the bill. And he knew a good story when he saw it. I remember looking at Mike Scaccia – who was still alive then – and Mike looking at me and it was clear as day that both of us were thinking the same thing.

You fucking dick.

But that was years later. Right now, the band have dropped me in Dallas and I'm heading back to Chicago on the train. It takes days, but I like to travel, and I'm off my tits. At first, at least. Then I start coming down, and it's a hard hard comedown. Because I can't avoid the truth that I'm going back to nothing. I've been slung out of Ministry on my arse. I've got no money, I've nowhere to live, and I've got no job. I haven't a hope of getting back in crewing with Jam till I get myself cleaned up. And I'm nowhere near cleaned up.
Nowhere near.

I'm back to kipping in Medusa's, and – however hard I tell myself I want to try to avoid them – all around me there's drugs and liquor on tap.

Much as I like to see the positive side of things, I'm in a bad place, and I know it.

Luckily for me, the Lollapolooza tour ends before I've had too much of a chance to fuck things up further, and Joe Kelly comes back to Chicago. Looking back, it's clear Joe plays a big part in hauling my life out of the fire at regular intervals, although – being the fool that I am – I never thanked him for it. At the time, I didn't even recognise what he'd done for me. I couldn't. But I can say it now.

Between that first Ministry tour and the Lollapolooza fiasco, me and him have started fronting a band called The Beernutz – we took our name from the packs of beernuts you get in bars, and used the logo too – and we've a regular gig at The Metro. Joe's singer and guitarist, and I play guitar. A guy called Herb, who runs a famous bar in Chicago called the Liars' Club, he's in it too. Even now, the band's still going, Joe's still in it, and they fill the Aragon on St Patrick's Day, every year.

So, Joe comes back to Chicago, sees what's going on – that I'm dossing down in Medusa's again – and invites me to a party to meet some friends of his out in the 'burbs. He knows he needs to get me out of where I am, away from the city, even if it's just for a few hours, which might – if we're lucky – stretch to a weekend.

His patience and his loyalty are something else. Before Lollapolooza, he got me away from the grasp of a drugs gang and into Scaccia's house to clean up. Then he watched me go from being off my head on coke to being wired on crystal meth, running straight from one woman with drugs to another one with different drugs. He knows that – whatever he does – the chances are he'll haul me out of the frying pan and I'll jump right back into the fire. And yet still he tries.

And in doing so, he saves my life. Again.

The party in the 'burbs is at the house of a woman called Monica. I go along, get friendly with her, work the magic. The party ends, but I don't go back to the city. I stay in the 'burbs with her, which changes everything.
First – and most important – the drugs aren't there on a plate anymore. I can't walk round the corner and into a bar and find whatever I'm after. This means that I start to level out.
Secondly, Monica doesn't cut me any slack. The devil finds work for idle hands, and she knows it. Right from the start, she's on at me to get a job.
Pretty soon I'm working at a warehouse out there in the 'burbs. Stacking shelves in a tool shop at night, which is horrible, but straightens me out. I guess – given what's been going on for the past few months – that's just as well. Being clean helps me get a job back at Jam, too. Compared with where I was a little while before, life is looking good. Really good. This means it's only a matter of time before I'm itching to play in a band, because that's why I came out to the States in the first place. Life in the 'burbs might be doing me good, but it isn't what I dream of. I live to play guitar. I'm still playing with the Beernutz, whenever I can, but that's not enough. I want more.

And that means auditioning again.

I start trying out for bands. It has one or two interesting moments. One time, the band I'm in have travelled to New York, and we're sitting in a room waiting to go in and audition, when Anthrax walk in. They look at me. Then take a second look.

Hey, you. You're that guy off the Ministry video, the guitar player.
Er... yeah.

Anthrax play a few Ministry songs, so they've been watching the live videos and studying me, and they're happy to sit down and chat. The other guys in my band are awestruck. *It's Anthrax!!!* and the guys in Anthrax are equally in awe of what I've done in Ministry, and I'm just happy to be there. The band don't get the audition, though.

Then I do an audition for Pegboy, which was the brainchild of John Hagarty, the guitarist from Naked Raygun. This gig, I really want. They send me a tape, and I learn all the songs on it. I've got them nailed. I know I'm going to get this gig. Then I go to rehearse with the band, and nothing I play fits in. My tape deck has been playing the songs at the wrong speed and while I've learned all the songs note perfect, I've learned them all half a step down. So that doesn't work out either.

Life in the 'burbs rolls on.

Every now and then I go into the city to work for Jam, or play with The Beernutz, and – sometimes – while I'm there I cut a little loose, have a little dabble. But it's just a dabble. Because it's not on a plate like it was when I was in Ministry, and that crazy oriental girl isn't there with a bag of crystal meth.

That stuff put a dent in me. Once you've gone a few days with that, you've *got* to have it just to stand up. Because you haven't slept, and you're exhausted, and you don't want to face the crash, and you *do* want to chase the high. So you have some more. And then you don't sleep. And then you need some more. And then – three or four days into the madness – someone throws a firework in the mix. And we know what happens then.

I'm never going back there, I tell myself.
I'm never going back.

casey orr

I reckon I first met Tezz when he was playing guitar on tour with Ministry, probably around '89. I was in the band Rigor Mortis, and my guitarist, Mike Scaccia, was also playing some shows with them. I remember thinking Tezz was a crazy Brit with a penchant for *bevvies*, so we hit it off right away!

Later on, I was bass tech for Ministry on Lollapalooza '92. Tezz came out with us for a few days and I ended up rooming with him one night. Of course, he was restless and went to wander the hotel. Didn't take him long to pull a table scrap, and I woke to his rutting in the bed next to mine.

Next morning the girl started freaking out because a baggie of 'stimulants' had gone missing from her saddle bag. She was upset – someone was going to be murderously upset with her if she was unable to produce aforementioned powder. Being the fine, helpful lads we were, we tore the place apart looking for her shit. At one point Tezz gave me one of his boyish winks and I knew what had happened.

The poor girl became so distraught at the prospect of the fate in store, that even Tezz started feeling sorry for her. As we continued 'searching' Bones said *If we find it for you, you'll share a bit, right?* Through her tears she said *Yes, of course!*

Lo and behold, the small baggie flew forth from Tezz's pocket onto the floor! *Is that it??!!* She was so relieved and, well... so stupid, that she never questioned the miraculous re-appearance. We received our well earned reward and headed off to the bus, feeling proud of our good deed for the day.

Years later, while I was playing bass for GWAR, I went to see The Business play in Richmond, Virginia. At the bar I noticed the guy next to me looked quite a bit like Tezz, although a tad heavier. I said to him, *You look like a fatter Terry Bones,* and he replied *I am a fatter Terry Bones!* I hadn't recognized him, and he hadn't recognized me – my hair was short at the time, and he had only seen me with long hair and, later, dreads. After hugs, bevvies, and a rousing set by The Business, we invited the band to stay at our house for the night. We had a great time! Mickey Fitz immediately made friends with Boris, my black lab, and spent most of the evening playing with him.

Tezz noticed my wife's hot sauce collection and challenged me to a test of tolerance. Being from Texas, I gladly accepted and let him pick the sauce. He chose one called *You Can't Handle This Hot Sauce.* It had a picture of Satan pointing his finger at you on it, and we each had a couple of drops on a cracker.

Holy shit! It was like a volcano on our tongues! We locked eyes, drawing every ounce of willpower we had not to break, as we watched the other slowly turn redder and redder and finally purple!

After an excruciating 20 seconds or so, Tezz finally broke, first lapping water from the sink faucet, then downing gulps of milk, before finally cramming a handful of sour cream into his gob! No time to revel in my victory, I quickly followed suit to quench the Hellfire in my mouth. Ahhh, fucking good times!

Sum Tezz up in a word? *Frisky!* Love the guy!

Regular Guy

Joe Kelly has been a good mate who's pulled my nuts out of the fire more often than I care to remember. But suddenly I'm out in the 'burbs and I'm not seeing much of him any more.

Why? Because Monica doesn't like us hanging round together. She knows what happens when I go back to the city to hang out with Joe. When I'm out in the 'burbs I'm the regular working guy she wants me to be. The instant I pick up my guitar and head back to Chicago to play in The Beernutz or hang out with my friends, that all goes out of the window and it's goodbye to regular working Tezz. I have a drink and a dabble, and another drink and another dabble, and all of a sudden I'm all fucked up and she doesn't see me for days.

She doesn't like that at all.

It's the classic situation. She sees my best mate as a bad influence, even if he has saved my life and brought us together in the first place, and decides I need to stop hanging out with him. So she turns on him. Whenever Joe wants to bring me back to the city to hang out, she puts a damper on it.

Joe looks to me for support. Waits for me to choose having a laugh with him and my Chicago mates over a steady life in the 'burbs with Monica. But I know that if I do that I'll be out on my ear again, and I don't want to be out on my ear. I think about dossing down at Medusa's and I shudder. So I sit on my hands and say nothing. I side with her, over him. Which I'm sorry about. But right now, this stability is what I need, and when push comes to shove I drop my friendship with Joe.

Maybe it was some kind of reward for making what Monica saw as the right call, the sensible choice, but she gets me a job driving for her folks. Her parents have a company supplying linen to airlines, and every day I'm doing the run to O'Hare, busy being a regular working guy, delivering baskets of fresh linen, and picking up the dirty linen to take away. Every morning I wheel these huge baskets of linen onto the tail-lift, fill the truck, then drive out to O'Hare, listening to the radio and offering heartfelt thanks to whichever genius invented the tail-lift and saved me from a world of pain, because the baskets are huge.

All in all, it's not a bad job. But it's winter. And winter in Chicago is cold. One day I get to O'Hare, park up, go to unload the truck, and the tail-lift won't work. It's so cold, the hydraulics have frozen. But the linen still has to be delivered.

The huge baskets have to make it from the back of the truck onto the loading bay so the ground staff can take them away. I've worked at Jam, unloading trucks and setting up gigs, and I'm used to physical work, but this is another level of graft entirely. Each basket has twelve big blue parcels of linen. Just one of those big blue parcels weighs more than enough. A whole basket is really fucking heavy.

I'm on my own. I back the truck up to the dock, and – one by one – I lift the baskets onto the dock. It's slow, it's heavy, it's hard. Part way through, I feel something tear inside. The pain is incredible.

Stuff the baskets, I'm off to hospital. That's how fucking bad it is.

I get an appointment and walk in to see the doctor. He listens to my story, gets me to drop my trousers, and takes a close look at my crotch.

Uh-huh. Thought so.
What, doc?
Yep, just as I expected.
Er, what?
It's a hernia.
A hernia?

He has plastic gloves on.
He's feeling around my groin.

Yeah. A hernia. There's a hole right about – and he pushes his hand in – *there.*

Fuck's sake!!!

I swear I can feel his hand in the back of my throat. It turns out I've literally bust my balls trying to push the baskets up from the truck to the dock. I make an appointment for surgery so I can get it fixed, but then life gets in the way. I never get the hernia fixed. I'm still nursing it now. I'm in no big hurry to have a doctor stick his hand into my guts just to show he can.

Delivering linen has suddenly lost its appeal. And anyway, Charlie's got in touch. He's found me via Karl Morris, who's living in Wisconsin, and he's rung to tell me The Subs are coming over to the States on tour.

He wants me in.

In fact he wants me to put the band together for him. A US touring band for the UK Subs. I get Matthew McCoy – who used to play in the Subs and who's living in Wisconsin – in on drums, and then I get Monica's cousin in on bass. He's never played in bands before, but he's a phenomenal classical guitar player, so I know he can do what I want, and probably do it in his sleep. Sure enough, I give him a bass, he learns the songs, the job is his.

Charlie flies in, we pick him up at the airport, bring him to the house in San Diego where we're going to start the tour. We have one rehearsal, and it goes like a dream. Next day, we're off!

The tour is great.

Good fun, we make some money, and it's good to be back on the road. We even find time to record a single with Nicky Garrett, the original guitarist, when we're out in San Francisco. He writes the song, we turn up, play it, Charlie sings. Bang. Job done.

I'm back doing what I do best, which is playing punk rock, and I'm loving it. But that isn't going down too well back home in the Chicago 'burbs.

Saints

Monica's not happy. She can see me slipping away. I've come to the 'burbs and dried out – more I regular guy out of me, I'm off, running back to the thing I love best. Music. And she can see there's going to be no end to it, because while I'm out on tour with The Subs, I get another idea for a band.

Battalion Of Saints.

The band was made up of the same musicians as on The Subs tour, except for the singer of course. Instead of Charlie, I contacted George, who I'd known since 83. He lived in San Diego. I gave him a bell, winging it, like I always do. Would he be up for it? Yes, he would.

While I was sitting in the van on my way from one Subs gig to another – none of your plush-but-flammable Ministry buses on this tour – I wrote the songs for Battalion Of Saints. Just structured the tunes in my head: verse chorus middle 8 guitar solo verse chorus verse end. Then I ring George again.

I'm coming through San Diego on tour, mate.
OK...
I've written these tunes.
Right...
Let's get in the studio!
Hell, yeah!

By the time we get to San Diego, where we've got a day off, the studio's already booked. We spend our day there, recording Battalion Of Saints. It might seem a weird thing to do, halfway through the Subs tour, but I was killing two birds with one stone. My thinking was simple: get the songs recorded while we're in San Diego, so that by the time I get back to Chicago the record is out, and then I can come back to San Diego, get the band together for rehearsals, and we'll go off on tour. And that's exactly what happened.

The Subs tour ends, and the Battalion Of Saints record is already out, on Tang records from Boston. They're run by a guy called Curtis, who's just moved out to San Diego. He's there, George is there, I'm starting to spend more time there too. And Monica's less and less pleased. I pop back to the 'burbs for long enough to say *Hi* and do my washing, and as soon as that's dry I pack all my backline, fly it out to San Diego, and get ready to start another tour with this new band. It's not what she has in mind for our relationship.

Battalion Of Saints go on tour. Monica's cousin is loving it, because all this is new to him and he's enjoying everything about it. Matthew and George? They're not so keen, because they've been around the block a few times, and what they see is us taking a big risk. And yeah, they had a point. I knew it was a risk, too. But my objective was to play in as many bands as I could before I got too old to do it. To make as much music as possible while I still had the chance. We were a good band, we played well, we did a lot of good gigs.

But financially... financially, the tour didn't do so well. We weren't making enough money, and we had an old van which kept breaking down and eating the cash we did have, which never does much for morale.

I was OK, though. I was playing music, and making use of the collection of backline I'd built up over my time in Chicago. After the first Ministry tour, when I'd had money, I'd kept my eyes open for anything that was being sold off cheap by mates, or mates of mates. Some of it I... acquired. Because I wasn't always too fussy about where it might have come from, but it meant I now had a full Marshall guitar stack, a small bass rig, and a set of drums. So I could put a band – like Battalion Of Saints – out on tour. I had a feeling that would be useful, and so it proved.

The tour ends in San Diego, and I fly back to Chicago. Monica's not best pleased with my new lifestyle (which is the same as the old lifestyle I had before we met) and I know I'm skating on thin ice. But I work the magic, and patch things up, though it's hard to be sure for how long. Anyway, my mind is on other things. Battalion Of Saints might not have had the successful start I wanted, but it has opened doors to more adventures. I'm only just home, and I've got another tour coming up.

The Business, who've just signed up to Tang Records, are coming over to the States on tour. Battalion of Saints are on Tang, too, so we get the support slot.

This is going to be good.

Business

The first Battalion Of Saints tour hadn't worked. We'd gigged all across the US, living in a van and hoping to make the money to eat and get to the next gig, but the cash was never there. Eating often turned out to be optional. Now we had a second crack at things with The Business tour, and I was determined this would be a different thing entirely. This time I was going to be on a wage. Both bands were using my backline, and I demanded that meant I got paid.

So far, so good.

Except this tour goes tits up as well. We're about a quarter of the way into it, when George the singer quits the tour. *Sorry guys, my wife's having a baby.* And he's off, back to San Diego. With no singer, the rest of the band go *Fuck it.* And that's the end of the Battalion Of Saints adventure. It's done. But I turn round to The Business and tell them *I'm coming with you.* And they agree. Because I'm the man with all the backline.

It's not a surprise that the others had enough and left. The trouble on this tour is outrageous. Every single night.

You see, The Business are an *Oi!* band from south London, and this means that – in the US – their fans are skinheads and nazis in all their various factions. The Hammerskins and so on. They haven't come to disrupt the gig – they're there because they're genuinely fans of the band – but opening the show in Battalion Of Saints was a hard ask, and not for the faint-hearted. Why? Because we're a hardcore punk band, and the audience response to what we were doing is a whole-hearted *Fuck this!* So we're on a hiding to nothing, every night.

Each gig is the same. It starts with us having a shit time. Then The Business come on and it all gets a whole lot worse.
They hit the first note of the opening song, and... it's fight time! Instant riot! Different factions are fighting each other, laying into each other. Rucks kicking off here, scraps erupting there. Fists and boots wherever you look. Some nights it gets so bad it spills over onto the stage, at which point the band decide the only thing to do is scarper. Then there's only me left, busy trying to rescue my backline while the nazis are picking it up and hitting each other with it. So I'm fighting them for that.

Fun.

Occasionally, just to add to the excitement, some nut job would set off a flare. If that wasn't enough, sometimes I got hit by rounds of ammo. Bullets that people had thrown at me. The first time it happened – while Battalion Of Saints were still on the tour – I came off stage and said

Someone's just thrown a bullet at me. What's it mean?
The bullet?
Yeah.

Er... that's a death warrant, Tezz.
A death warrant?
Yep.
Wow. Everyone's a critic, eh? Guess I needn't worry about playing in tune.

No-one else got one. Just me. Apparently, it's like a death card. Because they've killed people before in the hardcore scene. The Hammerskins have killed people. But then I'd get into rucks with them trying to protect my backline, which didn't endear me to them. And I think they knew who I was, and that meant they knew I wasn't from the *Oi!* scene, and I wasn't a skinhead.

They didn't like that either.

I know a lot of people – seeing the violence and the grief there was at the gigs – would have done what the rest of Battalion Of Saints did, and gone *Stuff this.* But I didn't care. I stuck in there. I pursued it. Because it's my job. And don't forget, this one was an earner. I got paid every night, so why not?

OK, I got a bit of grief. More than a bit. But then I get grief everywhere I've been. So, this wasn't so different. Water off a duck's back, and with all the fights you can handle.

Finally, the tour ends. Remarkably, my backline is all in one piece, and so am I. The Business are flying back to the UK out of O'Hare, which means my backline – which I'd flown it out to San Diego for the first Battalion Of Saints tour, the one where the van kept breaking down – is now back in Chicago, too. I've got money in my pocket and I'm back home.

It's time to go and patch things up with Monica, have a rest, and catch up with Joe. I know I'm going to have to be a regular guy for a while, but I know I'm not taking a job in a warehouse. I'm not going back to the truck driving either. Partly because I don't actually have a licence, but mainly because I don't want another hernia. One's enough.

I meet up with old friends, I have some nights out, and I get back in at Jam. It's all good.

Six months later, the phone rings. The Business are coming back to tour the States again, and they've a question for me.

D'ya want to play bass?

What can I say? The answer – of course – is yes.

More Business

Big Arthur Billingsley – of the Lurkers – had been playing bass for The Business before, and he hated it. *You can have the fucking job, mate, I'm sick of it.* So I was in. I knew the band, they knew me, and we got on. They also knew I had backline they could use, and that I'd fight to protect it if – or rather when – I had to. That clinched it. The job on bass was mine. And I was on a wage, again.

Better than that, playing bass with The Business was a doddle. I was getting $100 a gig, and I could have played the music in my sleep. Sure, I still got bullets thrown at me from time to time, but I can put up with a bit of grief for $100 a gig. The bullets were just part of the deal, because whenever The Business toured, the skinheads and the nazis were always there. They always have been. They always will be. In the States, The Business are branded with that, and there's nothing they can do about it. They'll do a gig and there'll be people going *Sieg Heil* and all that shit. Hundreds of people doing that. It's weird. And they're not nice to look at. They're ugly people. Scary ugly people. Big humungous tattooed guys full of hate. For fuck's sake. All you can do is take the piss, laugh at them, never back down.

How you doing, kid?
What?!
Got any more bullets for me?
Fuck you!
I'm making a bullet belt. Come on, you got some?

You see, nazis were nothing new. Back when I was still living in Stoke, before I ever moved to the States, I'd been involved with Section 5. I was playing bass with The Subs at the time, and I needed another outlet, something different. Section 5 were an *Oi!* band from Stoke On Trent, and I helped write their album Street Rock'n'Roll, doing guitar, but just in the studio. Some time after that, this huge festival – The Big Event – was organised for all the *Oi!* bands, down in London, and Section 5 were on the bill, along with the Angelic Upstarts, The Business, and a bunch of others. I went along to play guitar. And Ian Stuart showed up, with dozens of his followers, up in the balcony, giving it the *Sieg Heil*. And when the Upstarts played they poured down and there was this horrendous battle between them and the band and the crowd.

Like I said, big humungous tattooed guys full of hate.

So I wasn't afraid when I was playing for The Business, not at all. It never occurred to me. Safety? That wasn't an issue. It wasn't as if the band were nazis. They're regular blokes. Pissheads, actually. It's just the guys who come to the gigs. The ones who want to hit each other over the head with my backline, and lob bullets my direction.

I played with The Business for the next few years. They'd come over to the States every six months or so, we'd climb in a van and go off on tour, and I was always on a wage. Playing music, having fun, and making money. That isn't bad, whichever way you cut it. Although things could sometimes get a bit... lively.

On one of The Business tours – and I can't remember which one – we're doing a gig in Denver. We've borrowed a motorhome from Mark of the Antiheroes, and we're travelling round in that. We've done the soundcheck for the Denver gig, and I want to go backstage. There's a mexican guy standing on the backstage door, at the bottom of the stairs. I want to go up. He asks me for my pass. I tell him we haven't received any passes. He tells me

No pass, you don't go upstairs.
I ain't got a pass.
No pass, no entry.
Come on, man. Listen to my accent. I'm with the band, let me upstairs.

But he's a jobsworth. He isn't having it.

I can tell from his tone of voice this isn't going to end well. And while we're talking I see him slip a big Maglite torch down his sleeve and into the palm of his hand. And I figure he's going to clock me with it. So I get in there first. Headbutt him, and walk away, out to the motorhome.

In the motorhome, there's a party, with Micky Fitz as a genial host, mixing cocktails and holding court. I decide I'll stay here. Then there's a bang on the door. A friend of the band opens it, and through the open door I can see the mexican with a couple of mates. They've come to dust my clock. It's clearly time for round two. I step outside and realise the mexican's mates are big guys, and all three of them have baseball bats. *Hmmmm.*

Then someone on the bus hands me my pool-ball-in-a-sock, which I always have with me. I swing it round a couple of times, and say to the guys

Well, this makes it a little more even then, doesn't it?

The odds have just changed, and they don't like that. The mexican legs it. I hit another guy on the back and shoulders as he's running away. For some reason the big guy who was standing behind me didn't take the chance to hit me, which was a mistake. He should have.

I turn around and hit him hard in the side of the head with the pool ball. Really hard. Not soft, hard. The ball went *clonk!* like I'd hit a wall or something. He just stood there, and I thought

Fuck.

And then he dropped. Which was a relief. I didn't think about whether I'd killed him or not, I just got back on the bus, sat down and poured myself a drink. I was about halfway through it when a huge hole opened up in the side of the bus.

Someone's fired a shotgun at us, and it's like a bomb going off. There's a dozen people on the bus, drinking and partying, with the music blaring, and everyone hits the deck.

The driver's freaking out, which is fair enough. Micky Fitz screams at him *Put your fucking foot down and get us out of here!* and as he does, another hole opens up in the driver's door. The driver takes Micky's advice, puts his fucking foot down, and we take off.

Everyone's wound up and scared and angry. We drive to a friend's house and evaluate the situation. We know we've got to go back to the venue and sort this out so we can pick up the rest of the band – because there's only me and Micky on the bus – which will be tricky. We're also fairly sure the gig isn't going to happen, because the shotgun blasts suggest the venue security have crossed us off their Xmas card list for good.

We give it a few hours for the dust to settle. Then we go back to the club. The first person we see is the mexican. We chase him, catch hold of him, and hand him over to the police, who've finally shown up. And we check.

The gig is definitely off.

We drove the same vehicle for the rest of the tour. Just put a sheet of metal over the holes in the side of the bus, and carried on. If anything, we thought it was funny. It wasn't our responsibility, after all.

Although Mark might not have seen it that way.

steve whale

Tezz – we called him Bonesy, by the way – was playing guitar in Battalion Of Saints when The Business toured with them in the States. Obviously, with him being the english connection between the bands, we naturally gravitated to be really good mates. It was a natural progression when he started playing with The Business, and he slotted straight in without hesitation or a skip of a heartbeat. In terms of seasoned pros, if you asked me to pick a better member for The Business, I don't think I could. Tezz was like the missing piece in the puzzle in terms of making that band so rock'n'roll it would even have impressed Lemmy.

You see, we were legendary on the circuit for our partying and our bar bills. Micky Fitz was in full-blown addiction, being shot at was nothing unusual, insanity was our everyday norm. The only way I can describe what was going on is that we were already on the highway to hell. As soon as Tezz joined us, we doubled our speed. That's the long and the short of it.

If I told you what went on, you wouldn't believe me. The majority of it I can't really repeat, but this one time we played Denver. It's a hot day, the dressing room is downstairs, and the most stunning blonde girl is there with this summery dress on. What she was doing at a Business gig, I don't know, because it was a rarity to see someone at our gigs who had two eyes and a nose in the right place, so Tezz is straight in there, being all amorous, giving her the talk, rubbing her leg. She was happy to chat, but she didn't really respond to his advances. I didn't think much of it.

Then it's time for the gig. Someone says *Right, band's going on stage. Everyone out, time to clear the dressing room!* I'm standing there with my guitar, doing some warm-ups on it, and I look at the girl as she's going up the stairs. She's got a wooden leg. Tezz has just spent fifteen minutes rubbing her wooden leg wondering why she wasn't getting excited...

Then there was the Warped tour, 2001. At the time, nobody would give us a record deal, no-one would put us on. But Warped took a chance on us, and gave us two or three weeks on their tour. The very first day, after the show, they have a barbecue for everyone before they drive to the next venue. Micky Fitz gets drunk, steals a scooter, and runs the stage manager over. He has a choice between hitting the tour bus and running the stage manager over, so the stage manager gets it. Micky knocks him up in the air, and off he goes to hospital.

They draft in another bloke to take his place. Next morning, Tezz goes to use the toilet. The door's jammed, so he kicks it in, not knowing the replacement stage manager is in there doing his business, and smashes the guy's knees in with the door. That's The Business' start on the Warped tour: two stage managers sent off to hospital in 24 hours. After that, we were invited not to come back....

For me, Tezz is part of the history of The Business. The biggest part of it, and I can't say enough how much I appreciated him being on the other side of the stage from me.

Split

This is how it went for the next few years. Every time The Business came over, I toured with them, playing bass while nazis threw bullets at me. In between the tours, I went back to Chicago, worked for Jam, and made an increasingly fragile peace with Monica. But that couldn't last for ever.

One time I come back off tour, and Monica's finally had enough. As far as she's concerned, it's time for me to clear what little stuff I have out of her house. It's fair enough. I'm back chasing the rock'n'roll dream again, which means I haven't been thinking about her, or about being a regular guy. I'm doing whatever I want, and the years we've been together don't come into the equation. When I'm away on tour, our relationship doesn't count. I've worked the magic as long as I can, and for a while I've got away with it – there was no internet then, people weren't posting gossip and photos on social media – but Monica's started hearing things, and it doesn't look good. Two can play at that game, and while I've been away she's got another fella. Unfortunately, it's one of my mates. So I've got to move my stuff out of the 'burbs, move back into the city, and find somewhere to stay.

We were together a good few years, me and Monica. She helped me back on my feet when I needed it, and even though I chose her over Joe – which I felt bad about – I didn't regret it. Anyway, Joe and I were mates again now. He understood what had happened and why. Without that relationship with Monica, I wouldn't have straightened out, wouldn't have met her cousin, wouldn't have formed Battalion of Saints, or got this regular gig with The Business. Now I'm on my own again, but nothing lasts forever. Whatever happens next, I know I'll get back on my feet.

In typical Tezz fashion, I do. Kind of.

I'm no sooner back in Chicago than I hook up with the drummer in the Beernutz. Leanne. She's the first woman I'd ever played with in a band, and she was far and away the best. A phenomenal drummer, and gorgeous, too. I've stayed friends with the Beernutz while I've been out at Monica's, and now I'm back in the city we start hanging out together, and before too long I've moved into her place and we're in a relationship. On top of that, Jolly Roger knows he can trust me to work – and that I need it – so I've lots of work at Jam, doing festivals and the like. He's come through for me, I'm seeing Leanne, I'm back in the city.

Life is looking good.

Thing is, though, in this time I'd been introduced to crack cocaine. You might think I'd have learned my lesson after seeing where coke and crystal meth had led me, but no. I wouldn't say I got hooked on it, necessarily, but I was smoking a lot of it. And that's expensive.

It might have got even more expensive, but I had a tour with The Business coming up, which meant

I hadn't got time to get really deep into it. Before that can happen, I'm off on the road again.

We're doing the Vans tour, which is a humungous tour a bit like Lollapolooza, but with skateboard bands. It means we're playing to kids, not nazis, which is a bonus, because the kids don't throw bullets. By now – unless someone pings me with a bullet – I don't really pay attention to what's going on around me. I just put my head down and play the gig. I'm there to do my job. Look like I'm enjoying being up there, even if I'm not, because it's a job, and you've got to do a job right, else you don't get any more work. There's no mystery to it. Just do what you're paid for, and don't fuck up.

The Vans tour was a good one, no doubt about it. But then I live to be on stage, so in my book even a bad tour is good. Vans was fun, and it got me away from the hard partying. I'm not saying it saved me from a short life on a crack pipe in Chicago, but it didn't do any harm for me to get away when I did. You see, something always turns up. Always. However bad things are, there's always something around the corner.

Sometimes it's good, sometimes it's bad. This time... well, wait and see.

The tour gets to Texas. A guy from another band has told me his girlfriend lives in Houston, and that she'll bring me a package when she comes to the gig. It doesn't take a genius to work out the package is going to be drugs, and before you know it I'm back at hers, and we're having fun, and doing way more than just the drugs.

I don't even go back to Chicago. I stay in Texas, and get all my stuff shipped out. This was where I was going to start again. That may seem crazy – given that I had friends back in Chicago, and steady work at Jam, and a thing going with Leanne – but I always feel the need to start again, and I felt I'd done all I could in Chicago. I didn't want to work a normal job, and be a normal person, and I could feel that creeping in. I could feel myself getting a little bit too comfortable, and I'd rather throw everything away than get sucked into that. It was time to move on. To walk away, close that chapter of my life, and start something new.

So I move to Houston.

And turn the page onto a whole heap of trouble.

Houston

I can't remember what time of year I moved to Houston, because you never get a winter there. It's not like Chicago, where winter makes sure you know it's arrived. Houston just goes from hot to warm and back again. I remember sunbathing on Xmas day the first year I was there, so I think I might have moved there at the end of summer, but it's hard to be sure. The city's new and modern and full of oil money and cowboys, but I was living with this girl – who earned her living as a stripper – out in an old shotgun shack with a bunch of other old shacks. It certainly wasn't Chicago.

The moment I landed in Houston, I went looking for work. There didn't seem to be much happening musically that I could get into, and I tried working security – like I'd done at Medusa's – but that didn't go too well either, so I jacked it in. What I was looking for was a Houston version of Jam, and I found it. Kind of. It was a company who provided all the PA and lighting for events, but they were a bit more of a cowboy outfit than Jam had been, which was hardly a surprise. We were in cowboy country, after all.

My third or fourth job with them is at a hotel in Houston. There isn't really the sense of teamwork there'd been at Jam. The guys I'm working with, well, we've just been thrown together as a crew. We don't really know each other or anything. There's no real sense of teamwork either, and I know right off the bat that the kid they've put me working with is a stoner. He isn't co-ordinated, he's got a lackadaisical attitude. But I figured *What can he do wrong? We're only packing stuff up.* I'm paid to do what they tell me to do, I'm paid to turn up and do the job. That's it. We're just packing gear away after some event in the hotel. We'll be fine.

I'm working with him on a balcony in the hotel, which looks down into the foyer. During the event, they've provided lighting for the foyer by standing sections of truss on end at intervals along the balcony. At the top of each piece of truss there's a big heavy moving light attached to one side. This means the truss is both top-heavy *and* has the weight off centre, so – to stop the whole thing falling over – there are sandbags stacked on the plate at the bottom of the truss, making sure it's stabilised and held in place. It's a bit mickey mouse, but safe enough if you do it right. Do it right, and it's not going anywhere. But whether you're putting it up or taking it down, it's all about teamwork. You take your time, you work together, and you never – never – go pulling stuff away on your own.

We've already taken one of the trusses down further along the balcony, no problem, and I'm busy doing up the latches on the case we've put the light in.

The lad bumbles along to the next piece of truss and starts moving the fucking sandbags, without a care in the world. Nonchalant as you like.

I can't believe what I'm seeing.

I run across and try to grab the truss, but it's already tipping as the weight of the light pulls it over the balcony. The lad doesn't move. He just stands there, being stoned. No help at all. I'm doing my best to stop the truss going, but the weight of the light and the momentum and the gravity of the whole fucking planet are all against me. There's nothing I can do. The truss and the light are going over the balcony, and if I don't let go, I'm going over too.

There isn't even time to scream *Look out below!*

The truss and the light topple over the balcony and down to the foyer two floors below. There are people down there. It lands on three of them. I think it kills a couple. I hear it land, but I don't want to look. All I can think is

Is that my fault? Is it my fault because I let go??

The day has gone to shit and then some. There are cops and medics everywhere. It's tools down, stay where you are, we're going to need to speak to you, we've got questions. Work is done for the day, but that's the least of my concerns.

I've had friends die along the way – quite a few, that's the nature of life – but that's very different from being involved in an incident where people get killed. I've never ever spoken about it, because I just don't like thinking about it. I don't know *how* to talk about it.

Did I do enough? But I couldn't do anything else. I put everything possible into holding that truss, but there was no chance, no fucking chance of stopping it falling. And the kid? He just stood there. I don't think he even realised what he'd done. The two of us never spoke about it. And – after that day – I never spoke to anyone else about it either.

When I was interviewed about the incident, I told the main boss exactly what had happened. I didn't want to make it seem like it was the kid's fault too much, but – at the same time – what could I say? There was no way round it. I didn't want to land the kid in it, but as I said to the boss *The bag got moved. I'm not saying he did it intentionally, but the bag got moved, and by the time I got there it was too late, and there was no fucking stopping it.*

I never saw the kid again. I don't know whether they threw the book at him, or whether he decided it was time to disappear, to move town and get stoned somewhere new and lie low. My boss offered me another job, a better paid one, so it was clear he knew I'd done my best, that none of the blame for what had happened belonged to me.
But I didn't want a better job. I closed my eyes and I saw the truss tumbling through the air, and I heard the screams as it hit the ground. I didn't want anything to do with work now.
I just didn't want to know.

A few weeks later, that would be the least of my worries.

Speed

I'd moved to Houston to make a fresh start. Now, just a few months in, I'd been involved in an incident where people had been killed. Try as I might, I couldn't get past that. It didn't matter that the police had given me the all-clear. It didn't matter that my boss had made it clear he knew I'd done everything I could to stop the truss falling, and it didn't matter that he'd offered me a new and better job.

None of that counted. I shut myself away in the house, and blamed myself for what had happened. I told myself I didn't do enough, that I should have managed to do more. I beat myself up for not keeping a closer eye on the stoner. I told myself I should have gone over the balcony with the truss. I closed my eyes and I saw the truss tumbling through the air, and I heard the screams as it hit the ground.

All that kept on rattling round my head, and I couldn't deal with it. So I did what I always do. I turned to drugs. And because the woman I'd moved down to Houston to be with had access to speed, that was what I took. I didn't want to leave the house and face the world, so I stayed in and took speed. Whether she was there or not didn't matter. I was going to take some speed and then – in a little while – I'd take some more, and I'd keep repeating that till... Well, till something happened.

And something did.

I'd been up up for days, speeding, speeding, speeding. The dancer's gone off to work, and I hear a noise from the back room. Some guy has broken in. He's levered the window open with a knife – a big old Bowie knife – and he's climbed in through the window at the back of the house. I go through, and there's this little hispanic guy who thinks he's broken into an empty house, which means he doesn't expect to see me. That's definitely to my advantage. He's no idea I'm there till I clonk him one.

But I've been up for days, and I don't hit him hard enough. He comes at me with the knife. He's on speed, and he wants the speed there is in the house. I'm on speed, and I don't want him to have it. The fight is going to be loud and fast, but it's never going to last long. Luckily, it's me that gets the better of him, not the other way round. I grab the knife and I stab him, more than once. It seems entirely possible I've killed him, which – in my wired, frazzled state – is kind of what I'm trying to do, because that makes perfect sense. There's no shades of grey here. Not in my mind. It's kill or be killed.

Then I hear the sirens. The neighbours have heard the commotion, and they've called the police. The cops burst into the house, guns drawn, and the next thing I know I'm face down on the floor with my hands cuffed behind my back. Even then, I don't realise I'm in deep shit. As far as I'm concerned, I'm defending my home, but apparently that line of defence isn't going to work, even in Texas. There are several reasons for this.

One: I've stabbed the guy multiple times.
Two: I'm wired on speed.
Three: the police find more speed, the speed I had every intention of taking till the little guy wrecked my day.
Four: it's not my home.
Five: just no, Tezz, it's not acceptable.

As far as the cops are concerned it's two idiots fighting. Both the idiots are drug-addled, and one of the idiots has stabbed the other. I hear them talking to each other as I lie on the floor with the cuffs biting into my wrists, and the penny begins to drop. This is not a good situation. Not at all.

The guy gets taken to hospital, and I get taken to the station, booked, and stuck in a holding cell. There's a load of other blokes in there too, and then the speed crash comes on. I'm in a cell where there isn't room to lay down, and – more importantly – where I can't let my guard drop for an instant. I've got to keep my wits about me, and stay aware of what's going on, because the last thing I can do is show any sign of weakness or vulnerability. Do that, and I'm prey.

I'm there for days while the police try to figure out exactly what happened and what they're going to do. The hispanic guy's family want me charged, even though he's been stitched back together and is going to be fine. The dancer washes her hands of me. I never see her again. At some point – and I'm so disorientated by lack of sleep and the comedown off speed that I can't really remember what happened – I'm taken out of the holding cell and into a courtroom. I stand before a judge. The case is outlined. People talk. The judge listens, asks questions, makes his decision.

He sends me to jail. On remand.

Jail

The first time I'd visited Texas I'd managed to get myself locked up in a holding cell for three days in Lubbock. That scarred me. I didn't believe anything could be much worse. I was wrong. It could. Being in jail made that holding cell seem like a holiday camp. I've never talked about my time in prison before. In fact I've tried to block it from my mind, because it's got to be the most horrible thing I've ever come across.

I was on remand for three months before the case ever went to trial. Locked up in a cell with two other guys. In the films, prison garb is orange. Ours was mauve. I guess the thinking is it's about as un-macho a colour as you can get, so you're heaping embarrassment and shame on the men who are wearing it. I just knew it was really uncomfortable. What material it was made out of, I couldn't tell you, but it was rough and scratchy, and more like wearing a potato sack than clothes. The food was shit, too. I lost some weight in the time I was in there. As for a toilet, well, it was there in the corner of the cell the three of you shared. And there was a camera in each cell, too, so every time you took a crap a guard in some control room would be watching.

Even in the cell, you had no privacy. But within the prison it was the least dangerous place you could be. Which was lucky because that was where you spent most of your time. You spent all your day in this small, spartan room with two other guys, locked away and lost in a big, brutal institution full of the noise and smell of incarcerated men. Strip lighting everywhere. An exercise yard you might get in for twenty minutes a day, if you're lucky.

But none of that really begins to tell you what it was like to be in there. And I don't have the words to explain.

After three months of living with the stink of other people, the case goes to trial. The guy I stabbed survived – which was a relief else I'd still be inside now – so I'm charged with whatever they call *Grievous Bodily Harm* in the US. I plead guilty. It's the only thing to do.

I'm sentenced, convicted, and sent back to jail to serve another five months.

Five more months of keeping my head down and doing my best to blend in. Because you really don't want to stand out in any way. It's the exact opposite of how I've lived my life on stage, where it's all about showing off. Here I have to start again. Normal rules do not apply. I've already lost my english accent so I don't attract attention, and I know I can't relax either in the cell or outside, because if you open up about yourself or share anything about yourself, that'll be seen as a weakness. And that will get used against you.

It was a horrible place, that prison. Horrible. Scary horrible. There were thousands of men in there. And every one of them was in a gang. They had to be. You had to join a gang or you were fucked.

Every bit of your existence behind those walls you were vulnerable, because the law in there was violence. Unless you became a part of something, unless you affiliated with one of the gangs, you were dead, because without someone to protect you, you were just meat. You can't survive that place on your own. It's impossible. If you're not some kind of superman, you'll fucking die.

It divided on ethnic lines. Depending on your background, you became a member of black power, mexican power, or white power. The way it works is this. You're locked up. You're in a cell, you end up talking to your cellmates, they're members of the gang. You're roped in. You get protection. They get... whatever they want. In my case that was standing with them when there was violence with other gangs. And that happened every day.

It was horrible.

They were hard times. Three months on remand, locked in the cell. Then five months after I was sentenced where they put me to work in the kitchens, washing dishes. Each day a matter of keeping my head down, showing no weakness, and fighting when need be. Each day dragging. Each day knowing I was one day nearer being free.

A lot of my life I've been lucky. But prison put the dampers on things. This was one time when I didn't get away with it, didn't skate away from a situation, didn't have anyone to talk me out of the back of a police car or out of something I'd done. Like I say, it was more horrible than I could ever have imagined, and the only way I coped with it was to push it out of my mind and never tell anyone.

My parents never knew.
No-one ever knew.
Till now.

Eight months after I'd first been put on remand, I walked out through the prison gates and was free. The dancer was long gone, nowhere to be seen. I had nothing but the clothes on my back. I was on my own.

It was time to start again.

Freedom

The first thing I did was go to a thrift store. I've got a few dollars and the clothes I'm wearing, and that's it. No savings, no bank account, nowhere to live. I buy myself a Harley Davidson top to cheer myself up, and get in touch with friends in Houston who let me sleep on their floor for a few nights while I contact my parents and ask them to wire over some cash.

They don't know I've been in prison, and I'm not about to tell them. All they know is I ring them and tell them I'm skint - but it's just a temporary thing, you know - and can they send me some money to help me get by. They say yes, and while that's getting sorted out I spend a couple of days hanging with mates and try to work out what happens next.

I know one thing for certain: Houston hasn't been particularly good for me. Prison was hell. The only good thing I can say about it is that the charges I got convicted on never made it out into the wider world. Later, when the British authorities were checking out my past, they found my rap sheet from Chicago and Illinois - which was all minor stuff, and nothing to worry about - but they found nothing from Houston. Why? Because I was under the radar while I was there. Which is a blessing, because nothing I ever did - anywhere - was as anything like as serious as what happened in Houston.

I'm out of prison. Money is on its way.
The question is, what happens next?

Where do I go? What will I do?

I can't remember how it comes about, but somebody puts me in contact with Karl Morris. I'd heard that he'd left Wisconsin – he's nearly as much of a rolling stone as I am – but I had no idea where he'd gone. It turns out he's moved to Texas as well. He's over in Dallas. I ring him. We talk, and he says

Why don't you come to Dallas and play with Billy Club again?

This is the best offer I've got. By a long long way. Back when I was living in Chicago, I'd played in Billy Club one time. They were playing some place about an hour out of the city, and I just hopped on the bus with my guitar, caught up with them, and played along. I fancy doing that again, so when the money comes through from my parents, I take the bus up to Dallas and team up with Karl. I swap the floor I've been sleeping on in Houston for another one in Dallas, we do a couple of rehearsals, and that's it. We're ready. Billy Club go off on tour.

We're going to be doing a big tour supporting GBH, and as we drive across country to meet them we do some dates of our own to help pay our way, make sure we're really tight as a band, and break up the journey. They kind of set the tone for the whole of the tour, because violence was never far away. This is the tour of the Detroit Rumble, where GBH end up having to stop the gig for a massive ruck with the local nazis, but that was just one of many. One of many. Many many many.

I forget what drugs I'm on for this tour, but there are drugs. There's always drugs. In one form or another, there have to be drugs. I think I'm taking some kind of body-building steroid a girl had given me. I remember her giving me a big jug of them, saying *These will keep you going*. And they did. They were some kind of capsule, and they just changed my persona. Or let it loose, at least. Whether they were steroids or speed, I couldn't tell you. I just know they made me feel invincible. When they run out, the crash is horrible. But while I'm on them, out comes the Superman cape!

I'm in the mood that no-one's going to fuck with me already. I've just come out of prison where I've had to bury everything – my feelings, my hopes, and my fears – for eight months. Where I had to be ready to fight every single day. This tour is my release, and I know I need to go a bit mental. All that means I'm trigger-happy anyway, and now I've thrown these steroid-speed capsules into the mix.

If anyone wants to take the piss, I'll make them wish they hadn't. I'm fearless.

This is a complete change from tours with The Business, when I'd be stoic and concentrate on playing my guitar while nazis threw bullets at me. Billy Club go on stage, opening up for GBH, and as soon as any one person in that crowd says anything, I'm on them. Just drop my guitar, jump into the crowd, and start hitting them. In Atlanta, Georgia, there's a kid at the front, smoking. He deliberately blows the smoke in my face each time he breathes out, smiles, then turns and walks away. He's not gone far before I tap him on the shoulder. He turns round. I hit him. *Bam!* Sparks go everywhere. And then I climb back on stage and get on with the job, playing guitar.

There's lots and lots of fighting on that tour. Lots. Almost every night. But I'm fine with that. I've been penned up for eight months, and all the stuff I wanted to do in there but couldn't, all the anger I had to swallow because it wasn't safe to do anything else, I could finally let it out. Without the repercussions.

It's a great tour. We're all mates, we've known each other since 1980, we're all good lads. I enjoy it. And it's a decent-sized tour, too, which gives me plenty of time to get rid of all the rage and fury I've got bottled up. You'd have thought it might put some money in my pocket, too, but that didn't happen. I've never been any good with money. I do any kind of gig, and I do it for a pittance. That's why other people own their own houses, and I've spent much of mine dossing on floors.

All good things come to an end. And finally the tour with GBH and Billy Club is over. It's time for something new. So I move, again.

I'm going to Kansas City, Missouri.

ross lomas

I first crossed paths with Tezz on the *Attacked By Rats* tour. Our first gig was at Manchester Apollo. We walked in, all the backline was set up, and there was someone sitting at the drums, doing jazzy, bluesy stuff. *That ain't Wilf,* I thought. Obviously.

It was Tezz. I don't know how he'd got in, or what he was doing there, because Discharge weren't on the tour, but it was the middle of the afternoon, and there he was, playing the drums. And that was the start of a beautiful relationship. He hung around for the gig, we spent time with him after. There may have been a half a shandy, maybe a few more.

My memory's a bit cloudy....

He's always a good man to have on your team, always has a smile on his face. He's good old Tezz. But you don't want to cross him. In '99 we were on tour with Billy Club. They were on stage and there was some lad standing in front of Tezz, looking up at him, smoking. I thought *That's a bit weird.*

Tezz goes *Alright kid?* and grins, as he does, and the lad keeps looking at him. The vibes coming off him aren't good. He starts blowing smoke up at Tezz while he's playing, and then he walks off. I can see Tezz mulling it over in his head. He takes his guitar off, and walks calmly into the crowd. By then the kid is sitting at the bar. Tezz goes up to him, and the kid blows smoke in his face again. So Tezz just knocks him out, walks nonchalantly back to the stage, and carries on playing.

After the gig, he was back to normal, like it never happened. But I think he had to do a runner from the law that night. I think that may have happened quite a bit, one way or another.

Some days on that tour with Billy Club I'd wake up thinking *Ugh. What we doing?* and then I'd remember I'd be seeing Tezz. And the day got brighter, because that was always a good thing.

Because Tezz is a valued and treasured friend.

Nuts

Before I tell you about Missouri, there's a story from the Billy Club tour which – when it happens – reminds me who I am, and what I've done. Helps me remember I make music, and that I do it well. Puts the memory of that scratchy prison uniform a little further from my mind.

The tour supporting GBH is going to mean a lot of hours doing a lot of miles along a lot of freeways as we criss-cross the States. All in a beat-up old van. Luckily for us, we're old hands at making ourselves as comfortable as possible in a cramped space, and we know to stack our equipment so we've a raised platform someone can lie on while the rest of us sit and stare out of the windows, or drink beer, or talk about last night's gig. The usual ways of ticking off the long boring hours on the way from one gig to another that anyone who's done these kind of gigs will know.

As if the tour wasn't going to be long enough already, we've added some warm-up shows before it starts so we can hit the ground running, and these just add to the miles. We're based down in Texas, and these gigs help break up the long, arse-numbing drive up to Boston. Like I say, it's a lot of miles, especially in a van full of guitars and amps and drums, but that's punk rock, that's the music business at this DIY level, and that's what we do.

I can't remember where on the route it was – it was somewhere between Boston and Texas, that's all I can tell you, and that covers a lot of possibilities – but we play one of these warm-up gigs, Somehow, and for some reason I'm equally unsure of, we get into some kind of scuffle with some people at the end of the night. That's not so unusual. In fact, it's almost routine. Fists raised, punches thrown, egos bruised. Maybe a black eye and a broken nose or two. Nothing to see, or get excited about. The gig finishes, we pack the van, we go to where we're spending the night, and crash out.

Next morning, we set off for Boston. Dave the singer is driving. The rest of us are bleary-eyed, thick-headed, and already waiting for the moment we climb out of the van at the end of the journey, because that can't come soon enough. Ahead of us are hours of staring through the window trying to keep the boredom at bay, and we know it, and it's starting to lose its charm.

What we don't know is that – today – boredom really isn't going to be a problem.

You see, the folk we got into a ruck with last night weren't happy about what went on. And while we slept and snored and scratched our balls, they spent a little time loosening the nuts on one of the front wheels on the van. Maybe they meant for us to make it a few yards, make a turn, and come to a grinding halt. Maybe they just wanted to teach us a lesson, let us know we shouldn't have fucked with them. Maybe they really didn't care. Who knows? The point is, we set off for Boston, and the wheel stays on the van, and we haven't a clue what they've done. Right up to the moment where the wheel – literally –comes off. We're speeding along the freeway, and the first inkling we have of some kind of problem is when the fucking wheel parts company with the rest of the van. Suddenly, we're watching the front right-hand wheel decide to go its own way, shoot off at an angle, wave us a cheery goodbye, and plough down an embankment towards some houses.

We look at each other. We've got bigger worries than where the wheel's going to end up.

The van lurches, there's sparks and flames shooting out from where the wheel hub is grinding along the freeway, and – however hard Dave tries – steering the van is just about impossible. We know we're all going to die. Any moment now Dave's going to lose control of the steering wheel, the van will spin and flip, or roll down the embankment to join the wheel, and when that happens, we're done. The roof will fold down on top of us, and the amps we're lying on top of will fly through the air, crushing heads and breaking bones, and there's nothing we can do about it. We're screwed. And we know it.

It's strange what the mind does in these kind of situations, how those seconds stretch out into what seems like hours, how you react to that level of threat. I remember picking up an empty packet of crisps and asking *Who's eaten all these, then?*

I mean, what was I thinking? I'm sure the others were looking at me, wondering *What the fuck are you on about Tezz, you tosser? Fuck the crisps. We're all going to die.*

I never get an answer to my question. And it really doesn't matter. Because somehow – and god knows how he did it – Dave keeps the van upright, and on the road, and gets it to stop. We climb out. Take a deep breath. Try not to feel sick. Light a cigarette. And swear and swear and swear. The bearings and the hub where the front wheel should be are ground flat. Dave is the hero of the hour. We owe him. We promise him beer, women, oceans of alcohol. He's kept us alive.

We're alive!

Then we realise we're going nowhere.
And we swear some more.

We're standing by the side of the road wondering what to do, and what happens next, when this Highway Patrol officer drives up, pulls his car in behind us, and puts on the flashing lights. This isn't a good development. We all know cops aren't good news. This one gets out of his car, and we notice he's a bit young. Maybe that'll make things less difficult. Then again, it could mean he's full of piss and vinegar and a hatred of freaks, and it won't.

He walks over and asks what's happening. We explain. We show him the flattened hub. We point back down the embankment where the wheel went, and off into the distance where it's making a break for Canada, or a bar. We shrug our shoulders, agree we're lucky to be alive. Then – and god knows who he's talking to when this happens, or how it comes up – someone mentions that I played guitar for Ministry.

No???!!!
Yes.
You're kidding me!!
Honestly, officer, we're not.
This guy here?

The cop points at me.

That's the one.
You. Come with me. Now.

He walks back to his car. We follow. He opens the door, leans in, and turns up the stereo. Ministry blares out. This cop is spending his working day listening to Ministry as he's driving down the freeway, helping the hours pass. Our accident has made his day.

Next thing you know he's taking care of us. A local garage owes him some favours, so he rings them up and calls those favours in. The garage come out and collect the van, we wait there shooting the breeze with the patrol cop while the van gets fixed, and just four hours after the incident of the missing wheel we're back on the road and on our way to Boston. All because I'd played guitar in Ministry. And who, of any of us, saw that coming? It's crazy.

That's the thing about my life.
These things happen.
You just couldn't make it up.

Kansas City

The Billy Club tour finishes and I move to Kansas City. Why? Well, first off, there was nothing to keep me in Houston. I'd moved there for a girl, watched a lighting truss topple on people's heads, got in a fight with a speed freak, and ended up in jail. I'd gone there with hopes and ended up with nothing but the clothes on my back, so it's fair to say my memories of Houston weren't particularly positive. A fresh start was in order, and I'd found somewhere to make that fresh start.

When Billy Club had rolled into Kansas City, on the tour where I'd been letting out all the anger I'd had to bottle up while I was inside, there's a little interlude from all the fighting. I meet Elena. We get to talking. It turns out she's a dominatrix. *Hmmm, I think. I need someone to keep me in shape.*

Before too long, I'm looking at naked pictures of her and making plans to move to Kansas City. It shouldn't be a surprise – it's what I do. When I met Christine I used that as a reason to move from Stoke to Chicago. When that went sour, meeting Monica got me out of Chicago and into the 'burbs. I moved back to the city when I met Leanne, and down to Texas for the dancer.

Even I can see a bit of a pattern in that.

It's time to see what Missouri is like. I move up there, and move in with Elena. She's got a nice house, loads of money – there's clearly a good living to be made as a dominatrix – and life in Kansas City is nuts. In the first flush of excitement about being together, Elena and I get married. Then I put the feelers out for work with The Business (and anyone else who wants a guitarist) and get myself a job working in a restaurant to put a bit of regular cash in my pocket. I'm back working in the kitchens, the same as I did in jail, but this is a restaurant doing Louisiana cajun cuisine, so the similarities with Houston stop right there. I like this job. It's ok. Hard work, but I'm used to hard work. This is a hard grafting job, and when you're working in kitchens you can't go in there half-cut, which means I knock the drugs on the head too. Taking a break from the steroid speed of the Billy Club tour will do me no harm at all. New city, fresh start, and all that.

Before I know it, I'm back playing in bands again, and all is well. I'm back touring with The Business when they come over, which is usually once or twice a year. On top of that, my good mate Mark Magee – who works doing their merchandise – is in a band called Anti-heros, based in Atlanta, Georgia, and I'm helping them out on bass. They're touring with Agnostic Front and they need a bass player, so I step in. I really enjoy it, because Mark's a good friend – who's still out in the States now, working as a tattooist in Atlanta – and I even do some gigs where both me and him play guitar. Sometimes I get up on stage and jam with Agnostic Front, too, although I'm never a member of the band. All in all I've plenty of opportunity to go out on the road and make music, which is great. After all, it's what I'm best at.

Even when I'm back home in Kansas City, I'm in a band. Of sorts. Because Elena has bought a drum kit. She's bought the most expensive drum kit you've ever seen in your life, and she wants me to teach her how to play so that we can put a band together. I give it my best shot, but – whatever her other qualities – it's clear she's not a natural drummer. After weeks of practice with this all-singing all-dancing kit we eventually get to a point where she can play one little pattern on it.

I say *It doesn't matter, we'll use it*. Confidence is everything, and she's determined to play the drums. We put a band together. We do a couple of gigs. Elena decides that she's going to make up for her lack of ability by playing the drums wearing her dominatrix gear, which should at least take the audience's mind off how she hits the drums.

It's not a bad idea, love, but you might have to leave the shoes off....

So, we do these gigs. We even record a couple of tracks. It's not brilliant, but it's ok. And in comparison with the last few years, this period of my life counts as incredibly stable. I've a job working in the kitchens, and every now and then I head off on tour. That's good. Sure, when I'm not busy with either of those, I fall back into old habits. Sport bores me, I don't read, and the devil finds work for idle hands.

On days off, I drink a lot and take a lot of coke. As always.

Then I decide to make a visit back home to Stoke. All the time I've been in the States I've only made it home to see my folks every every two or three years, because my life is chaotic and money is scarce. But this spell in Kansas City has put cash in my pocket for the first time in a while, so I book myself a flight and fly back to catch up with my folks.

And doing that changes everything once more.

Loose Ends

Whenever I came back, I was reminded how cold Stoke is. I might have grown up there, in a house with an outside toilet, but I'd got used to life elsewhere. To America. Chicago has a proper winter, but it has a summer too. In Stoke, you get a lot of cold. Winter, spring or summer, it's freezing fucking cold. I'd come back a few times over the years – whenever I had money in my pocket and felt the urge – and it always came as an unwelcome surprise. I'd see my folks, and I'd tick off the days till I flew back to the States. Occasionally, I'd catch up with people I knew, and something more would come of it. One time, in the days when I was playing with Ministry, I flew back from Chicago and met up with Tosh, the singer from Section 5. He got me to play guitar on their album. The next time I came back, I did it again.

This time, I'm here because I owe my folks a visit for wiring over the money when I got out of jail. But that's it. Stoke isn't home, and I know I'll be ticking off the days until I leave.

Then it turns out Nigel – the guy who played bass in Discharge for those first few gigs so many years ago – is having a party. I go along. All the band are there. Me, Bones, Rainy, Calvin. We have a few drinks. We have a few more. We chew over old times. We make each other laugh. We drink. We talk over each other. We get loud and ridiculous and we keep on drinking. And at some point I say

We can't let the band die like this. We should get back together. We're all here. Let's do it.

I'm drunk. I haven't thought about what I'm saying. I'm just going with the moment. But some part of me knows that if I don't say it, none of them ever will, so I might as well. I open my mouth, the words spill out unplanned, and the idea is out there. It's been said. All I'd meant to do was fly over and see my folks – I didn't know about the party and I never expected to end up drinking with the guys – and now this has happened. Is it complete luck? Or the complete opposite? I don't know. I have another drink. Time will tell.

A day or so later I fly back to Kansas City. Back to Elena and my job in the kitchens. The job doesn't seem that good any more. Too much graft, too little fun. Elena isn't as happy with me, either. She's still around, but I can see her thinking about making a change. Then, all at once, it happens. She packs her bags and heads off to Florida, to someone with more money. I'm gutted. And just while I'm dealing with that, my cellphone rings. It's Calvin.

Tezz?
Yeah.
We'll do it.

It's the call I've been waiting for. I take off my apron and walk out of the job, out of Kansas City, and – where else? – back to Chicago.

I feel safer there. It's familiar. I've got people around me I know I can trust. And right now, I know I need that. I catch up with Joe Kelly, but he's an electrician now, with a good job and a young family, and other priorities in his life. We speak, but he's not going to risk blowing what he has by hanging around with me. Jolly Roger's still around, so I'm back in at Jam, working on the crew, drinking and doing drugs. Which means coke again. Not too much – for once – because I'm working as much as I can, so I don't have much free time to waste on it, but enough.

I'm hanging out with Scotty Death and Phil Cisco, living with them in their flat over the tattoo shop where they worked. They were mates from when I'd been in Chicago before, and when I told them I was coming back, they said

Come and live with us....

And how could I say no? They were all part of the scene, part of that big family of Jam guys and reprobates, but they partied a little too much to be able to work at Jam. They wouldn't have been trustworthy when it came to turning up sober, if I'm honest.

Life's good. I'm back in Chicago, in the part of town I know, where it's walking distance to Jam and the Aragon ballroom one way, and walking distance to the Metro in the other. I'm right where I want to be. I start seeing Leanne again. She still drums in The Beernutz, but I can't get back in – they've replaced me with someone good. Everything's fine, but I know it's only temporary, because Calvin's agreed we're putting Discharge back together.

Really, I'm just tying up loose ends.

My backline gear is in storage in Kansas City. I've left it there when I move back to Chicago, and I don't pick it up till I come back through with The Business one last time. It's backline that's done a lot of miles, and could tell a lot of stories. The Ampeg bass rig, the Hi-Watt set up with the Union Jack painted on the front I'd never asked too many questions about but was probably nicked, the Marshall stack Tang Records bought. And now I'm selling it off. The support band on the tour buy the bass rig, give me cash, put it in the trailer, and off it goes. Some punkers in Kansas City buy the Marshall stack. The Hi-Watt? Who knows. It doesn't matter.

I'm selling everything, and fucking off back to England. Except my guitars. Those I'm going to keep. Those are coming back to Chicago with me. Six Les Pauls, and I love each and every one of them. I've accumulated them over the years, they're worth a fortune, and they're full of memories. No way am I getting rid of those, I tell myself. But then I realise I'm moving around so much I can't keep them. It's only a matter of time till someone nicks them, and what's the point in that? I let three of them go.

It's time to move on. Time to get on the plane and go home. After all those years away, leaving in 1988 and coming back in 2002, I come back to Stoke with nothing to show for it. Just one bag of clothes and three guitars.

Full Circle

I know it's not much to show for all that time in the States. One bag of clothes and a clutch of guitars. But it was all I had. Sure, I had loads of memories - and quite a few blank spots where memories should be - but after nearly fifteen years away, you'd expect to come home with more, and I wasn't. That didn't bother me. Something was, though. I just couldn't put my finger on it. And it was only as I got on the plane that the penny dropped. I was coming back to Stoke with a truckload of mixed feelings. Maybe two.

The thing was, I didn't like leaving Chicago. I knew the place. I had work, I had friends, I had some degree of stability. And in my life, stability has been all too rare. Yes, there'd a lot of moving around, but I was used to that. I've always been like a gipsy. Yes, there'd been a lot of drugs, but I was OK with that, too. I know it'll seem weird to people who've normal lives, but in all that chaos what I had in Chicago still counted as stability.

Now, I was leaving that, and I wasn't so sure it was a good idea. I'd told myself I was coming back full circle to re-join the band it had all started with, to get Discharge back together and out on the road again. That had to be a good thing. But would it work? Could I make it happen? Was I throwing everything away on the basis of one drunken evening and a phone call? As the plane headed east across the Atlantic, I couldn't shake the thought I was doing exactly that.

Two days later, I'm living in the basement flat in Bones' house in Shelton. Just up the road from my folks. The best thing I can say is, it was weird. My folks were happy I was back, but Bones? I don't know. He didn't say much of anything. He didn't tell me what he'd been doing for the past fifteen years, and – to be honest – I didn't ask.

I wasn't here to be best mates with my brother, I told myself. I was here for Discharge. That was what counted. I'd deal with this by pretending it's just like the times I've come back before, when I'd visit my folks for a couple of weeks or so, and I'd ring Charlie and see if the Subs had any work for me – because sometimes he did – so that I could fill my time out on the road with them before I went back to Chicago, or wherever.

That was the plan, anyway.

To some extent, it works. Discharge do start rehearsing, and writing an album. And I carry on living in Bones' house, down in the basement, putting it all together. We've got the original line up. I'm on drums, Rainy's on bass, Bones is on guitar, and Cal is doing the vocals. It should be like old times, but it isn't. Cal and I haven't really rekindled our relationship, and the only time I see him is when he comes by at rehearsals, and even then he's holding back on the vocals. Over the years, I suppose, he's got used to doing things his way. It's not the same.

Me and Bones work on the album. There's no real input from the others, but – despite that – it comes together quite well. We produce an album called 'Discharge', which comes out on a decent label, but gets more or less shelved. As far as I can tell, there's no promotion for it, but I don't know why. I just know the album's released, but without any publicity. You can find it if you want to, but you'd need to be looking for it.

By now, I'm bored. And that's never good.

To get past that, I'm spending most of my time wired on speed. And drinking, too, because beer and speed go hand in hand. Stoke is turning out to be cold, and wet, and miserable, and I'm remembering why I left in the first place.
When Discharge get offered the opportunity to play Ozzfest, I put it to Calvin, and he says no. We could be taking part in this massive festival, but we're going to turn it down. I can't believe it, and yet I find myself thinking it really doesn't matter. I should be frustrated that this is slipping through our hands, but the truth is I don't care.

I'm too full of amphetamines.

I'd spent week after week being bothered about this Discharge reunion not being what I'd hoped. Now I'm living in the moment, doing what I do so well, and hiding away in drugs instead of thinking about making a plan, or sorting things out. I get up in the morning, and have a line. Then I open a beer. Then I have another line, and for the rest of the day it's beer and speed on the hour every hour. Speed's not expensive, but the cost is adding up, because I'm getting it in big bags, a couple of ounces at a time. Gigs are paying for it all. Occasional gigs with Discharge, odd bits and bobs with The Business. Europe, a tour of Japan, stuff like that. The only gig I turned down was when they went to Jerusalem. For some reason, I didn't fancy it. And sure enough, at the airport they got pulled apart by the Israeli authorities and the Customs men.

I was dodging bullets again, I thought. But the truth was I was hell-bent on self-destruction.

That was the only way I could deal with living back in Stoke. There was nothing to do. Nothing. After the US, life here was tedious. The weather sucked, and I had no-one to hang out with. I was bored and I was miserable.

At least speed stopped life being boring.

jeff juniak

I first met Tezz – briefly – in New Jersey in 98-99 when I went to watch The Business with a couple of friends. It all kicked off that night because Micky Fitz pulled out a St George's flag and started going on about England, and I don't think the American skinheads liked it very much.

Fast forward ten or eleven years and I'm living in Stoke, married to Bones's ex. She and I were always arguing and falling out, and I'd be regularly packing my stuff when she kicked me out. One time this happened, and I went up to the Red Lion in Burslem. Tezz was there. I knew who he was, obviously. He knew who I was because I was playing in another band at the time, and when I told him my situation he said *Come stay at mine then.* Which was pretty cool considering we didn't really know each other. So I went back to his house, and we got off our faces for three days straight. From then on, we became pretty good friends and started hanging out together. I started singing in Broken Bones, and then – as things evolved – with Discharge.

Tezz is an absolute one-off. If you want a story, here's one from the Broken Bones tour of 2013.

We're doing a gig in Brno in Czechosolvakia. It's a nine-hour drive, and the whole way there, Tezz has been going on about how he needs a shit, he desperately needs a shit. Finally we pull up at the venue, Tezz climbs out of the van, says *Oh man, I'm going to destroy that toilet* and disappears into the venue. He finds the toilet, does his business, pulls the chain to flush it, breaks something, and floods the whole fucking place. He's been in the venue five minutes, and already the whole venue is wet and stinks of shit.

It's vile. *Vile.*

I don't know what he'd been eating, but an hour or so later, he needs another shit. He's broken the toilet, so obviously he can't use that. The venue was kind of in the middle of nowhere. Across the road there's nothing but woods. Forest. And it's dark out. So Tezz decides he's going to have a shit in the woods. It's pitch black, you can't see anything, so hey, why not? Off he goes, into the trees.

Just then, some guy gets in his car to leave the venue. His car's facing towards the woods, and as soon as he starts it and turns the lights on, what do they illuminate but Tezz in all his glory, squatting down, having a shit. With the car headlights beaming right on him and a load of Czech punks going *Look! It's the guy from Discharge!*

The gig went ahead. It was far and away one of the smelliest gigs I've ever played. Tezz had literally destroyed the toilet. How's he get away with this kind of thing? He's very charismatic. He's got a roguish charm.

That's the only way I can put it. A roguish charm.

Drink and Drugs

It wasn't as if I was doing anything new – I'd always cranked life up a little with whatever was to hand. Cocaine, regularly. Crystal meth when I was on tour with Ministry. In Battalion Of Saints, truckers' speed. These little pills you can buy in any truck stop, hundreds of them in a container. Neck one or two of those with coffee, and they'll keep you awake on long drives. Take a handful with a beer or three, and suddenly you're off your tits. It'll be no surprise I tended to take them with beer. And it wasn't as if I was the only person who did this – almost everyone I knew took something, sometime. Everyone had their poison. The difference, if there was one, is that some people did it more than others.

Booze was always there, that was a given. And when you've been up all night drinking and taking whatever's to hand – because that was how things were – then sometimes things get out of control. And that's not just the bands. Audiences can be just as fucked up, too.

I've seen skinheads glassing people while I've been playing on stage. I've been at gigs where people have fired guns. That was in California. I mean, who takes guns to a gig?

That happened at a Business gig. Their gigs were just a big ruck every night because of all the different Nazi gangs, which was bad enough, and dangerous enough, and then – on top of that – idiots were bringing guns along and you could say the wrong thing and end up getting shot. That's messed up, whichever way you look at it.

Can you deal with that kind of madness when you're sober? I don't know. Getting off your chops seemed like the only thing to do – especially in California, where it's all gangs – but a lot of the time it just poured petrol on the flames. Back then, Micky Fitz was drunk 24/7 and – being a drunken idiot – he'd get involved with these gang leaders and they'd get him to do things. He'd be taking their drugs and they'd have a quiet word in his ear

When you're on stage, man, just say this.
Nah, do that.

Talk about lighting the blue touch paper. Micky would step up to the mic and say or do something and the whole place would just ignite. We might as well have gone out on stage with gunpowder and matches. One time, we played a sold-out venue in California and Micky made a U-sign with his thumbs and fingers. It's a gang sign for a gang called Unity, which is an anti-nazi gang who go hunting nazis.

He made that sign and the whole place kicked off. We never even got to play a single song, and Micky had no idea what he was doing or why it had happened, because he was pissed.

It was rare we had a gig where something didn't happen, because – sooner or later – drink and drugs bring chaos in their wake. Regularly, with The Business, we'd start playing, and Micky would walk out on stage blind drunk, giving it the big whatever.

Next thing you knew, he'd fallen over and hit his head, and that'd be it. He was done for the night.

Oh, for fuck's sake. Does anybody know the songs?

The same thing would happen with Tosh, the singer from Section 5. He'd get so drunk he'd just fall off his stool. Looking from the outside, that's pretty chaotic. Selfish, even. People who are busy thinking of themselves and nothing else. And maybe it is. But I wasn't in a position to point the finger, because I wasn't a saint myself. I just held it together better when I was on stage. Mostly, anyway. Because it was my job. Playing guitar was my job and doing it well meant I got paid, and that was all that mattered.

I just took whatever happened on the chin. The chaos, the rucks, the madness, even the guns. The way I saw it, if anyone attacked me, I could handle myself. I had a guitar in my hand, and I'd fucking brain them. I know that might not be everyone's idea of a well-thought out health and safety policy for the workplace, but it made sense to me. It was what I was used to.

Over the years, then, being round drink and drugs had become a normal part of life. Utterly unremarkable. There, like some people have toast and tea in the morning. You watch others fuck up, but you're sure you're not. You're good. You've got it under control.

You. Are. Not. Like. Them.

I was back in Stoke. I'd spent all the money we'd been advanced on the album on beer and speed. Calvin's turned down the offer of ridiculous money for us to play Ozzfest. I don't get it.

What does he mean, no?

Nothing makes sense any more. Only the speed helps. With it, I feel invincible. Without it, my life is careering downhill, spiralling out of control.

And it's only going to get worse.

Battered

In the midst of all this, there's a fight.
There always has to be a fight.

I've got a gig with The Business, playing a one-off gig in Japan. Rebellion. It'll be our second trip to Japan, it's a good earner, and it'll get me out of the UK – which means out of Stoke – for a few days. So that's all good. The afternoon before I'm due to fly out, I decide to go round and see my folks. It's a nice day, and I'm walking round to my folks' house from my flat, minding my own business, thinking of nothing in particular.

I'm wired, obviously.
These days, I'm always wired.

I'm walking past some roadworks – they're digging holes the length of the road, putting in new pipes, or checking old cables, or whatever it is they do – when a car drives by, slowly. These three guys are peering out the windows at me. I flip them the bird. The car stops. The guys get out. Three asian guys are squaring up to me and waiting for me to back down. But it's me. And I'm wired. I don't back down. *Come and have a go if you think you're hard enough!*

The fight starts. Right by the road-works, with all the workmen taking a break from digging holes and filling them in and resurfacing it again. They're watching what's going on – god knows how it looks to them – and we're the entertainment for as long as it lasts. Fists and kicks and adrenalin. I feel like I'm holding my own, and then one of the asian guys picks up a shovel that's lying on the ground, swings it, and hits me right in the knee. The force of the blow knocks me back in a hole in the ground, and they jump back in their car and take off.

I'd been doing all right till they hit me in the leg with the shovel. But as soon as they did that it was all over. I was off to see my folks and now I'm lying in a hole with blood pissing out of my knee. One of the workmen phones for an ambulance, but they don't give me a hand up or anything. As far as they're concerned, they've done their bit, and as soon as the ambulance turns up and the crew get me out of the hole and off to hospital, they'll get on with filling it in and covering it with tarmac. If that doesn't happen sharpish, maybe they'll leave me in there and fill it in anyway. They're not interested in giving evidence or saying what they've seen when the police turn up, either.

Dunno, mate. Just found him in the hole, bleeding. No idea what happened.

The ambulance arrives, ferries me straight off to hospital, and I have twelve stitches in my knee. They're right across the middle of my kneecap. My knee's all swollen, I can't bend it an inch, and the hospital have given me a crutch to use if I'm walking anywhere. If I come to a hill or a set of stairs, I've got to go up them backwards because trying to do anything else is agony.

There's no way I'm going to Japan. I ring Micky Fitz to tell him I can't make the gig.

Why's that, Tezz?
Well, someone's sliced my knee open.
Really?
With a shovel.
A shovel?
Yeah.
Right.

I can tell he doesn't believe me. He thinks I'm making up some bullshit excuse because I can't be bothered to leave my home turf and fly to Japan. I can't really blame him. I barely believe what's happened myself.

The Business head off to Rebellion in Japan, with someone else stepping in for me, and I limp around on my own in Stoke. It's a good few weeks before I get anywhere near being back to full fitness, or full mobility anyway. The guys? I never saw them again. Still haven't. The fight at the roadworks had been purely random – they were blokes, not kids – and if I hadn't flipped them the bird, who knows what would have happened? They might well have driven on, and I might have gone round to my folks, chewed the fat with them, and flown to Japan. Life might have been entirely different.

But, fuck it. That isn't what happened.

If there's a choice to be made at the moment, I'll get it wrong. I'm doing loads of speed, I think I'm invincible, and when I meet a woman down the pub and we start doing speed together and neither of us have got what you might really call a job and the devil finds work for idle hands so before you know it *bish bash bosh* she falls pregnant, I think

Let's have a kid, why not?

I told myself that my mom would be pleased, that I was – partly – doing it for her. My older brother had two kids, but I was sure my mom would want more grandkids. Weirdly, when I announce I'm going to be a dad, it turns out Bones is, too. Twins, doing the same thing at the same time. Bizarre.

Anyway, now my mom's got two grandkids on the way, and I'm telling myself it'll all be great. I couldn't have been more wrong.
The woman and I have a little boy, Jack Daniel, but she drags me down and I fucking let her. We're still doing speed, and everything – it, her, a lifetime of taking whatever's to hand whenever it's there – it all gets the better of me.
I drop the ball, big style. She tells me I can't be in the band any more if I want to see my son. So I split the band up, like a fucking idiot.

Because I've already fallen in love with my son.

Arrest

Thing was, if I'd had my wits about me I'd have known the relationship was doomed to failure. I should have known that she was bad news and we were bad for each other long before we had the boy. But I was too full of speed to see the blindingly obvious. I'd spent a lifetime running from one scrape to another, and every time something went wrong I told myself this was just one more scrape, one more bump in the road, nothing more. Even when the truth was as plain as the nose on my face.

Late in 2004, we had a fight. She was drunk and off her face, and I was probably no better, and we were arguing – as we did – and she attacked me. She punched me in the face and I hit her back. I punched her with my left hand, to stop her, and blacked both her eyes. That was it, the end of the evening. The argument had been nothing unusual – we were always sniping at each other – but the violence was. Even so, we went to bed. Together. I got up next day, and she was gone.

While I'd been sleeping off the booze she'd gone to her mother and called the police and told them I'd seriously and grievously assaulted her. First thing I know is when the police turn up at the house and tell me that. I just laugh, because I can't believe this is happening. Because it's fucking ridiculous. Because she hit me first.

The police aren't laughing.
They arrest me.

That might not have been the end of the world, but in my jacket pocket the cops find some live ammunition. Two live rounds. One's a 9mm, the other, something huge. I'd brought them back from America with me when I was over there with Discharge earlier in 2004 – when we went over to the US without Rainy – and we went out shooting in California. A friend of ours over there was a collector of guns, and one day we went out shooting. How often do you get a chance to fire a kalashnikov, after all?

It wasn't the first time I'd fired guns. I like guns. I had a Glock when I was in Chicago. All my friends had guns. In Texas they had assault rifles. I'd been in shooting ranges, but I never fired a gun in anger. And then we were in California, where you can just go out into the desert and fire at whatever you like, because you're in big empty spaces where anything goes. So that's what we did. It was a great day out, some fun, a bit of a laugh, and at the end of it I picked up a couple of rounds, stuck them in my jacket pocket, and never thought anything of it. And when I walked through Customs in the UK, I never got stopped. And there the bullets were, sitting in my jacket for the police to find.

They find these two bullets and make a big fucking hoorah about it. Ammunition's a bigger deal in the UK. The police think they've got a gun dealer or a bad man or something. More of them come round and tear the flat apart, check up the chimney and down the loo, look at everything and everywhere. It didn't matter that I told them I had nothing. What I told them made no odds. As far as they were concerned I had bullets, and I'd committed a serious assault on my girlfriend. I was a bad man, so what I said made no difference. In their eyes I was guilty.

I was put in the cells for three or four days and then the case went to court. My dad was there, and when they started reading out the charges he was shaking his head in disgust. This just proved what he'd always thought, that while I'd been my mom's favourite, I was nothing but trouble.

I was gutted.

I spent a few weeks in jail on remand, somewhere up north, and then they decide the only thing they can actually charge me with is common assault. Next to nothing. I plead guilty and get a conditional discharge. It's all over. Done and dusted.

You might think by now I'd have learned my lesson. But I'm too fucked up to know which way is up. I should have given her a wide berth, but I don't. After all that, I get back with her. Why? Because she's pregnant with my son.

Sometimes you have to go a long way down before you can bounce back. Like I say, she drags me down, and I let her. I quit the band. I keep taking speed. I say I'll do anything for my son. None of that matters, and none of it helps. When something's that fucked up you can't make it work. In the end, she wants me gone. The police get involved again, and I find myself in the cells for the night.

Again.

When they let me out I go to my mom's and stay there. Everything's gone. The relationship's over, I can't see my son, and I'm not in the band. I'm forty-four years old and I'm in Stoke, living with my folks. This wasn't how things were meant to be. I know it's going to be a long way back from here.

It is. But, little by little, things improve.

The manager at the Sugarmill venue is an old friend, and he asks me if I want some work. He needs a crew chief. It's sporadic work, but I enjoy it. I'm doing something I want to do, something I'm good at, something I enjoy. I'm catching up with bands, seeing them do their thing, and even if I don't like it, it's OK. It's money, and a bit of stability, and some kind of purpose.

For a couple of years that's what I do, and then Karl Morris gets in touch. Do I fancy going to eastern Europe with Billy Club? Yes, I do. I quit the Sugarmill, and head off in a van round Europe on a tour. Two weeks later I arrive back in Stoke with just £100 to show for it, and no job to go back to. That might seem like I was a prize idiot, who'd make a bad deal, but I didn't see it like that. Partly because I didn't know I was only going to get £100 when I said yes, but mainly because going out on that tour was therapeutic. Apart from a handful of gigs with Section 5 I'd done next to nothing for way too long, and this Billy Club tour reminded me how much I missed it.

I was still doing speed, but less of it. I had a bit of shape to my life. I realised that doing a lot of speed over a long time isn't clever. I was coming back from the depths, I could tell.

But I had to be honest with myself.

I'd always told myself and the world that I could handle anything, do anything, take anything and come out sunny side up. I was Tezz. The man who never took a backward step, and who always walked out of the wreckage unhurt and unscathed. Thing was, I knew that wasn't true. I'd known it for some time.

It was time for me to be honest about my past.

Toast Truth

It was 1984 going on 1985, and there I was, playing guitar in the UK Subs. I could just about pull it off, but I knew I wasn't *that* good. So I was under a lot of pressure, most of it from myself.

We did this gig – I think it was at *Gossips* in London, but it could have been somewhere else – one of those popular after-hours-get-together kind of places, wherever it was. And there's a fight. Some random bloke smacks a fella who's tuning my amp, and next thing the whole place has erupted in one big fight. That's it. The gig's over.

I'd been full of beans. I'd just started taking on the guitar like I wanted to, thinking I'm all this and all that, and then the gig goes tits up and I don't know how to deal with it. So I do what I do when I'm not happy. I take a shitload of drugs. I don't ask what it is, I just snort it all, and go back to Deptford's flat with him and Jim Moncur and a bunch of others, having a party. Then the drugs take control. Everyone's having a good time, and I'm sitting in the middle of them, having anything but a good time, thinking

What do I want to say? Who am I? How do I express myself? How the fuck do I tell people what I'm thinking? WhatdoIdowhatdoIdowhatdoIdo?

All of this is running through my head, over and over and over, and I can't deal with it. I want it to stop, and I don't know how to make it stop, and I can't handle sitting here if it doesn't stop. So I do the only thing I can think of to make it stop. I do what a northern nutter would do to make it stop.

I jump over the balcony.

And that nearly makes everything stop. Forever.

Luckily it didn't. Look at all the stuff I'd never have got done, all the adventures I'd never have had, all the places I'd never have seen. But that night at Deptford's I didn't know what to do and it was tearing me up, and I couldn't handle it. So, fuck it. Let's jump. Two floors up, over the balcony, down onto the concrete. That must have been a hell of a thing for them to see. We never spoke about it. Ever. They were stunned, I imagine. I was stunned, literally. But I am sorry about it. It was selfish, very selfish, and it must have been horrible to see. And I never thought for a moment they'd get arrested and blamed for pushing me. But I can't say this clearly enough. It wasn't them. It was me.

Was I really after toast that night? Maybe. That was all I ever seemed to eat, back in the 80s. But I jumped over the balcony because I was miserable and I didn't know how to make it stop, and when I woke up in hospital with my head the size of a melon and the police asked me what had happened, there was the plate of toast in front of me, and that was the first thing that came to mind. The only way I could think of to explain to the police that it was me. I did it. Not them. Me. And then I went back to sleep.

Deptford and the others were never really happy to see me again. After them being locked up and accused, that's hardly a surprise, is it? Because that was my fault. And we never talked about it, ever. I wanted to say sorry, but I didn't know how.

I had problems, as you can imagine. I couldn't communicate with people, because I didn't know how. It felt as though I was withdrawn from the world, like I was seeing the world through curtains or from behind blinkers. As though I was in a box. As though I wasn't really part of it. So I filled myself with drugs and drink, and kept going. But inside, I was numb. Emotionally numb.

I was literally numb, too, after that fall onto the concrete. All down the left side of my head. It didn't stop me playing the Lyceum a few weeks later – which was the first time I'd seen Deptford or Jim Moncur since they got locked up and accused of trying to kill me, so it was a bit awkward, to say the least – and it didn't affect the performance onstage, either. If anything, from there on, playing up to the northern nutter became the driving force on stage, because the northern nutter – this bloke daft and stupid and crazed enough to jump off a balcony because he wanted toast – was what I thought people wanted. And I wanted to believe it, too.

But in reality, it was taking its toll.

I was becoming hard work to be around. I wasn't well. I had the blinkers on. I was constantly rubbing the left hand side of my head because it was numb, and that was the least of my odd behaviours. I'd always been weird, but now I was more weird than ever, in an unusual way which people weren't expecting. I think it's fair to say the incident where I wrapped a warm turd round the tour manager's head showed that. I was substituting drink and drugs for not being well. Hiding myself in that. The blinkered feeling of being in the box hadn't gone away, and it wouldn't go away for a good few years.

So I decided to drink and take drugs to get out of the box for a bit, but that's not a solution for someone like me. Because however much you try to ignore it, the problem is you always have to get back in the box.

You sober up.
Or the drugs wear off.
And you have to get back in the box.

Clean

It's over four years now since I had a drink or took any drugs. I stopped on New Year 2014, and I've not touched anything since. What brought that on? A combination of things. My dad died. I met Sadie. And I knew I wanted to get back into Discharge and make a good go of it, sober, so there's no fucking up and I've got no-one to blame. Maybe my dad dying meant I did some growing up, I don't know. I just knew it was time for me to take some responsibility for myself.

Meeting Sadie kicked it all off. I met her through Tosh from Section 5. He texted her from my phone, and left her number on it. I'd seen her in passing, but never met her, never talked to her. But I took a chance and texted her, asked if she wanted to meet up for a drink. And we did. This was 2012. At this point I wasn't playing music, I didn't have a guitar, and I didn't really see the point of anything.

By the end of the next year, she'd got me back on my feet, assured me that life wasn't over, and that I would get back up. Above all, she helped me to give up drink and drugs. Although really I did it myself. Because you've got to really want to fucking do it. Only you can do it, and I decided this was the last crack of the whip. I had to shape up or give up.

There's no other way of doing things. Not for me, anyway. I had to just quit. Drop it all. It's hard, but what else can you do? You can listen to hundreds and hundreds of people telling you how they did it, how you can do it, all the rest. You can listen for forever and a day and... nothing. The only person who can make it change is you. It's only you who can make that decision. Just like that. *I have got to stop. I. Me. I have got to stop.* Only you can put it right. You start exercising. You start doing other things. And it's hard. No doubt about it. Especially at the start. There were some days when I looked at my life, and saw a lot of solitude. Days when I'd had more interaction with people while I've been in prison. There still are. But whatever. I'm not complaining. I've made my bed, and I'll lay in it.

I had to change my life because I knew I was getting old. There weren't a lot of bands I could play with any more, especially back here in England, and I wanted to be back in my old band, playing guitar, with a beefed-up sound, with a new guy singing, with new tunes. I wanted to take it on properly. That was it.

Wanting to get back in Discharge was a huge motivation. And I couldn't do that if I was drinking, because then I tend to fall out with Bones all the time. And I realised the less I put in the way of our friendship, the better it'd be. So, no drugs, no drinking. That's how it is. The rest of them can do what the fuck they want, but I'll just sit and watch them. That's what I do. How the fuck I do it, I don't know, but it's what I do.

It was horrible at the start. It's only when you realise you can't do it any more, that you understand how much the world revolves around getting wasted. The music industry is the worst place to try being sober, believe me. There's booze everywhere. A fridge in the dressing room, full of beer.

I've sat at a table with lines of speed and coke laid out on it, and everyone partying and going off to carry on somewhere else.

What you up to later, Tezz?
Going home to my wife and dog. What you doing?

But I'm ok with it. I've done all that shit. I'd like to think I've done enough to last me two lifetimes. I've gone over the top on doing everything I could possibly want to do, filling my boots, knowing that this time would come where I wouldn't be able to do it any more and I could reflect on that, and remember I've done a lot more than most people will ever do. And when it comes to a time when I can't do anything for myself any more – and that time will come, unfortunately – I can always reflect on that and know I lived my life the best I could.

And has it helped the band? Oh yes. Tremendously. More than I could ever have imagined. I mean, I had an idea things would improve, but it's been way way better. Me and Bones work well together now. He's rated as a phenomenal guitar player by a lot of people, there's very few who can play his style. And the drum pattern I came up with suits what he does. In the old days, we were always feuding over something or other. We'd go out of our way to find something to argue over. Back then we were always bickering. If it wasn't the music it'd be something else. I felt that I was the one who was thinking ahead, and he didn't. He seemed happy enough with whatever was there, and I wasn't. I wanted to move forward, push on, while he came along just for the ride.

I'm sick of fucking carrying you – why don't you forge ahead and I'll come along for the ride instead?

But that ain't gonna happen, it ain't never gonna work. And as you get older you understand why you're here on this earth. There's people like him and there's people like me. I'm not going to change his nature. I know that now. But at that age, back in the day, I wasn't going to sit back and say

Let me just think about this, let me just solve this problem by thinking.

No. I snorted this and drank that, and if someone wasn't on board with what I wanted then they were gonna fucking suffer.

Now, I'm sober. I've come full circle, but it's different. I'm not putting obstacles in the way, like I used to. Do I look back and think if I'd been sober with other bands earlier it might have been different? Yeah.

If I'd been less pissed on the Ministry tour, would I have set the firework off? Probably not. Would I have played more of the Lollapolooza tour? Oh yeah. Would I have ended up in half the scrapes I got into? Not a chance.

But what's done is done, and you can't change the past. And at least I've got some great stories.

The ones I can remember, at least.

sadie

If Peter Griffin and Lemmy were morphed together you would get Tezz. He is definitely one of a kind. He can be the kindest, most loyal and charismatic man one minute and a complete knob the next but life is never dull with him around that's for sure.

If I was to sum up Tezz Roberts in one word it would be this:

Feral.

Wrapping Up

I was 22 when I jumped off that balcony. Life's a little different now. I think about things, which I wouldn't have done then. Then, I was still a kid, who had everything he thought he wanted, right there. Drink, drugs, women. And I took it all, and jumped. That changed my life. If you fall two floors onto concrete, it's going to rattle your fucking biscuits, isn't it? But I like to think it enhanced certain things, too. It made me a little more get up and go, you know what I mean? I wasn't going to sit around and wait for things to happen, I was going to go and fucking get it.

That's the attitude which made me move to America, because otherwise I was going to be living with my parents in Stoke-on-Trent, and that wasn't happening. I'd watched how they'd had to lead their lives – my mom had spent her whole life in Stoke-on-Trent, cleaning in factories while my dad worked in the foundry – and I didn't want that for me.

Music was my way out. A creative way out. I never wanted to stand still. I believed something better and new had to be just round the corner.

If I didn't like what I was doing, I decided I'd change it. If I didn't like playing one instrument, I'd try playing another. Take Discharge. I started off singing, but I wanted to change the music, so I learned the drums. That way, I could drive the music that we made. I played the drums, but I got bored of looking at the rest of the band, at the back of their heads. I knew I wanted to show off. So I learned bass. Then I learned guitar. Changed bands. Moved from the UK to the States. Changed, and changed again. Kept changing.

My life – even now – is very much about looking forward to what's next rather than looking back to what I've done. Living on past glories? That's bollocks. I've always gone forward, never looked back. Don't get me wrong, I get why people reminisce. They go and see a band and want to hear the songs that remind them of being 19 or 20, because that's a great time to be alive.

You're full of yourself, and you haven't had to make compromises and learn to live with disappointment. Who isn't drawn to that?

I don't look on myself as being anything special. I just do what I do. Fortunately for me, over the years, I've built up a legacy. You can't buy that. You can't go into a shop and buy it. You've got to earn it. And I've gone out and earned it. Not many people have gone out and done what I've done, and are still around to brag about it. I never think about it, never reflect on it, I've just done what I've done because I had to do it, because there's fuck all else out there for someone like me. Once in a while, though, when I sit and talk about it, I realise I've done quite a lot.

I've gone and done it because I thought it was the right and only thing for me to do. And I still do. My life has been a series of highs, amazing crescendos, with proper troughs in between. Each time I've hit a low I think *Maybe that's it*. And then things pick up again. I can only think that's because it's meant to. I truly believe your life is mapped out. I can't think all these things have happened just because I wanted them to. But then again, who knows? It's not like I've never been wrong before.

Right now, Discharge are signed to Nuclear Blast. That's worked out really well for everyone. We've been all over Europe doing gigs and festivals, and toured America a couple of times. Unfortunately I couldn't get back in there, and Rainy couldn't either, but we didn't find that out till we'd wasted money applying for visas. Me and Bones decided the band would go anyway, and use the money made on the tour to pay off the bill we'd run up applying for the visas, so they went with Karl filling in on bass and just Bones on guitar. They did the tour, and they paid off the bill. Then they went back again and made some more money without me, which I wasn't too happy about. It bothers me, sitting at home while they're over there, when I could be seeing old friends, seeing old places. But what can you do? I've got to swallow it, and that's it. I've had to deal with worse things, you know.

I've played with bands where I've been a hired gun, and it's a job. You're just doing a job. But with us, with Discharge, it's mates and loyalty as well. And I'm enjoying it. I'm putting everything into it. I'm a lot more enthusiastic and positive about it all than I was a couple of years ago. Things are looking up, all the time. We've a new album coming out. The band's rehearsing, and Bones is full of ideas. The band's a lot harder, we're going out and giving people what they want. We've injected youth into our band with Jeff, and it's brought youth to our gigs. We've a young man fronting the band who takes his top off, jumps around, and gives them what they want. And it brings them in. It's bringing girls to our gigs. You look out and there's girls looking up at him, all wide-eyed. Perfect!

> We're in a good place.
> I'm in a good place.
> Back on the game.

I'm enjoying what I'm doing, and I'm excited by what I'm doing, and I'm fifty-six years old. Here I am, at this stage of my life and being happy, and I'm all together very grateful for it. I put my life on hold for music – and I wouldn't change that for the world – but it's been a pretty minimal existence, financially. When I get too old to make music, I've got nothing. I haven't got a pot to piss in, and I'll go out of this world the way I came in, with fucking nowt. I know that. But so what?

I've packed more into my life than most people would dream of. Job, security, family, none of that was ever for me. There's people who want that, and I understand that I'm the freak, the outsider, the odd one. I've got none of the rules and regulations that go with normal life, and I've got ups and downs they'd never dream of, but there's no safety net. Once you fall, you fall hard, and it's a bigger scramble to get back up. And that gets harder as you get older. The highs from getting to do what you want? They're well worth it. It's a struggle, but there's one thing to remember: confidence is everything.

There's been a lot of scraping by in my life. A lot of scraping by. A lot of drugs. A lot of women. And quite a few guitars. And always – always, always – there's been my mantra.

Confidence is everything.

And I don't regret a thing.

also from Ignite Books

City Baby

Ross Lomas has played bass in GBH for over thirty years.

In this best-selling autobiography, he tells his story.

Learn how punk rock, and love, saved his life.

On sale now at
ignitebooks.co.uk

Ignite Books is a small, independent publisher. This book is the latest in our series which we hope puts fresh, thought-provoking, entertaining writing before a new audience. We have a lot of fun doing this, but we also survive on a shoestring budget and a lot of graft. So, if you've enjoyed this book, please tell your friends about us.

You can also find us on Twitter @ignitebooks, so drop by and say hallo. And to learn more about what we do, or shop for our other publications, just visit our website at ignitebooks.co.uk

Thank you.